The Smiling Woman

By M.A. Edwards

Olcan Press

First published by Olcan Press on 5th September 2022

Olcan Print/Press are a subsidiary of the Olcan Group

6 Park Hill, Ealing

London, W5 2JN, UK

Email: team@olcan.co

www.olcan.co
Content copyright © M.A Edwards

For permission contact:
team@olcan.co

A CIP record of this publication is available from the British Library.
First printed November 2022.

Paperback
ISBN: 978-1-7391440-1-2

Contents

Prologue Cardiff

'Bloody Mary.'

Darkness stalked around the eerily quiet bathroom, with only a small shaft of light seeping through the cracks in the door to reveal the silhouettes of two girls standing before a large, ominous mirror. In the daylight, the mirror appeared like any other; but in the darkness, it adopted a sinister appearance that could make even the bravest man's hair stand on end. The girls turned from the mirror to look at each other, their eyes wide with excitement. The one girl boasted a neat blonde plait that lay down the back of her neck and trailed to meet her white dress. Her rich, dark chocolate eyes- almost the shade of coal in the shadowy room- were fixed to the hazel eyes of the other girl. The girl with hazel eyes stood slightly taller than the other, though the similarity between their facial features would reveal to any onlooker that they were indeed sisters. Six years older, the girl with hazel eyes had soft, tanned skin and deep red lips conveyed a maturity the other did not yet possess. In the years to come, she would have grown to become a beautiful young woman. Perhaps achieving her father's expectation of graduating from University and becoming a doctor. However, the cruel hand of fate had decided this young girl would not receive that chance.

The older girl turned back to the mirror, put her hand on the glass and closed her eyes. Her sister watched intently, a shade of fear sneaking into the chocolate pool of her eyes. She opened her mouth slightly as if to warn her sister not to tease, not to tempt, the dark and mysterious forces at work here but the silence stole any sound from her throat so that not even a whisper could escape.

They remained frozen in this position for a moment. One sister with her hand pressed against the glass of the mirror, and the other helpless but to watch. The older sister licked her lips and swallowed, preparing to begin.

'Bloody Mary.'

The older sister could sense her younger's fear growing, and this made her smile. She had never been a cruel sister, but sometimes she enjoyed having that little bit of power over her sibling. The two fatal words came to her sister's mouth for the second and penultimate time.

'Bloody Mary.'

Deafening silence engulfed the darkness once more. The shaft of light retreated to whence it came, suffocated out by the slithering shadows that circled the two sisters. A chill crept down the younger sister's spine, followed by a tear welling up in her eye. Her lower lip began to tremble as fear invaded every cell in her body. 'Please', she whispered, '…please don't'. The older girl kept her hand firmly placed on the mirror, however now the smile had spread across her face. That cruel smile reverted any sign of beauty in her face to an ugliness that her sister had rarely seen. The older sister bit her bottom lip, holding back the words and building the anticipation to a climax.

'Bloody Mary.'

Both girls stood motionless, every cell in their bodies alert. The only source of light in the room now observed from the haven behind the keyhole in the door handle. A solitary beacon of hope, which ordinarily would have fought against the waves of opposing shadows, now cowering in safety. The older girl turned her head to look at her younger sister again, her eyes bright with excitement and adrenaline.

'See, I told you, nothing to worry about! I knew nothing would happen. It is all a load of rubbish. You should have seen your face. I am surprised you didn't wet yourself you were so scared! Wait until I tell Jenny, I-'

Suddenly, the younger sister's face drained of all colour. Her rosy cheeks transformed to a light shade of grey and her whole body began to shake uncontrollably with fear.

'Stop it. You are only trying to scare me. Its over now, so you stop it.'

The terrified girl raised a trembling finger. Every hair on the older girl's body stood erect as a chill swept through her soul. The finger pointed not at her, but behind her. Slowly, her eyes followed the finger, passed where she was standing, to the mirror, where an icy glaze had crept over the surface. The older girl stared into the mirror, but instead of finding her own hazel eyes staring back at her, she saw something that made her skin crawl. A Woman.

The Woman's face was covered with a black veil, beneath which only a vague outline of her pale features was visible. Slowly-but with a grotesque grace- the Woman lifted a hand towards the glass of the mirror. The almost translucent skin was drawn back over the bones revealing blue veins that spread across her hand like spiderwebs. The fingers were long and crooked with black talon like nails protruding from each tip.

The older girl willed her hand to move from the glass as the Woman's drew ever closer, but no matter how strongly she willed it, it would remained fixed to the glass. Frozen to the thin barrier between her and the Woman. Like a fly trapped in a spider's web, unable to escape as it watches the spider creep towards it with it's fangs dripping poison as it edges closer and closer.

The Woman's claw-like hand came to rest on the mirror opposite the older girl's. The barrier could not have been thicker than a sheet of paper as the girl felt the coldness of the Woman's hand from the other side on her own. Her sister stood motionless, her breath freezing before her eyes as the temperature in the room dropped lower. A tear trickled down the girl's cheek and fell to the floor without a sound. The predator observed its prey with curiosity from beneath the veil. Waiting.

Then, as loud as a gunshot from the cover of silence, a crack echoed around the bathroom. The older girl, her hand still fastened to the glass, forced her gaze away from the Woman to the corner of the mirror. A small crack had appeared in the silver. A chink in the armour. A weakness in the only barrier between the sisters and the Woman.

The older girl could hear her heart beating faster in her ears, so loud that she thought the Woman must be able to hear it also from behind the invisible wall. The sound of fear.

Another crack.

The splinter in the glass crept towards the centre of the mirror. Tears escaped from her eyes and ran down the older girl's cheeks, falling to the floor.

Crack.

'No... no,' the younger girl whispered from behind chattering teeth.

Crack.

The older girl forced her eyes back to the Woman. She seemed closer to the glass somehow. So close that her breath would appear on the glass. However, no breath marked the mirror.

Crack.

The next moments happened in a matter of seconds, but felt to the sisters like a lifetime. The older girl willed with all her might for her hand to move from the mirror and, as if some higher power heard her plea, her hand was released, and she was sent sprawling onto the tiled floor. No sooner had her hand recoiled from the glass, the final, deep crack appeared in the silver. A deep, horrifying laugh of victory came from underneath the Woman's black veil. The Woman trailed one of her grotesque claws down the crack in the glass, unleashing a piercing scream into the room. She stopped where two cracks met and let her talon linger at the crevasse. The younger girl felt a whimper sneak from her mouth. The Woman's head snapped to the left to look at the little girl on the other side of the mirror. Raising the finger from the glass, she lifted it to her the lips beneath her veil and hissed 'Shhhhhhh.'

Transfixed, the sisters watched as the finger left her lips and the sharp needle-like end pointed towards them. She bent the finger back with a crack of her bony knuckle. The Woman's finger hung mid-air and then moved forward, allowing the girls to watch as the tip of her razor-sharp claw curve forward. She tapped the glass with the lightest of touches, but the wall shattered around them. Small shards cut their skin as it fell to the floor, marking them with thin red lines as the older sister instinctively grabbed her younger's arm and pulled her to safety in the corner of the room. The barrier had crumbled, however one thing remained. The Woman. Without a sound, the Woman stepped forward into the bathroom. Into the girl's world.

For a moment, the three figures remained motionless in the bathroom. The sisters cowered against the far wall of the bathroom as the Woman stood in the centre of the room with her black veil still covering her face and a long black shawl trailing slightly behind her across the sea of shattered glass.

'Please, please don't hurt us,' the older girl begged as she held her sister close in her arms. The Woman raised a long finger to her lips once more. 'Shhhhh.' Now the Woman was in the room, the command held more power and the older sister lowered her eyes to the floor in surrender. The Woman moved her finger towards the bottom of her veil and slowly lifted it over her head, revealing a visage that would haunt the girls for the rest of their lives- however short that may be.

The Woman's face in shape and features appeared almost human. A long, slender nose trailed down her face between two black, pencil-line eyebrows. However, it was at this point the Woman's similarity to humanity concluded. Her large, circular eyes were a bright white colour with only a small, opaque pinprick of a pupil in the centre that skated around the white in excitement. This was not the feature that caused the sister's heart to beat faster. From one side of her face to the other, the Woman smiled. A smile only featured in the darkest, most disturbing nightmares of the human mind. Her thin lips were of a dark grey colour, but where the corners of the lips should have been, a ragged, dark red line continued to the corners of her face-as if a razor blade had been dragged through her haggard cheeks. At the corners, yellowish blotches and black veins creeped away from the terrifying creation to her temples. Within the smile, the teeth had a disgusting golden tinge and accompanied the revolting stench of the Woman's breath.

The sisters pulled each other closer. A damp patch spread around the crotch of the younger girl's dress and her sister felt the warmth from this soak into her own trousers. Then, the Woman spoke.

'Do you think I am beautiful?' The voice, a low, grumbling that was almost unrecognisable, was as repulsive as nails trailing down a chalk board. The girls remained speechless; eyes fixed on the scarred mouth of the Woman.

'Do you think I am beautiful?' the Woman repeated in the same spinetingling voice. The younger girl looked to her older sister for answers but all she found was hopelessness.

'Answer me!' the Woman screeched, making the shards of broken glass vibrate on the floor. The Woman composed herself, 'Do you think I am-'

'Yes,' the younger girl muttered 'Yes, you are...you are beautiful.' She couldn't force herself to look at the Woman as she said this but if she had, she would have seen the grotesque smile grow larger. The

Woman raised a long, bony finger and beckoned the innocent towards her. The girl looked at her sister but her gaze still remained fixed on the tiled floor. Gathering her strength, she tried to stand but her older sister's grip was too tight for her to move. Prising the older girl's fingers off her, the girl stood before the Woman.

The Woman looked down at the young girl through her pinpoint pupils, her smile never wavering. With one of her claw-like hands, the Woman gripped the girl's shoulder and leant in so that her mouth was next to the girl's ear. The smell of her breath drifted through the girl's nostrils, but she controlled the urge to gag. A thin, forked, snake-like tongue emerged from the Woman's mouth and grazed the side of the girl's ear. When the Woman spoke, a new cold seemed to enter the girl's body- chilling her blood to almost freezing.

'I will make you beautiful...like me...' While the Woman whispered this into the girl's ear, a long, thin, pale, cadaverous arm emerged from beneath the shawl and a hand picked up a large fragment of mirrored glass. 'You are going to be beautiful...Just...like...me.'

Before either of the sisters could react, the Woman jabbed the shard into the corner of the young girl's dark, red lips and slid it effortlessly, like a knife gliding in melting butter, through her cheek. Blood gushed from the incision onto the floor as both girls let out a deafening scream in unison. Holding the captured girl tighter in her clawed grip, the Woman mirrored her actions to the other side of the face. The young girl's scream stopped. Only one scream remained.

The Woman dropped the slaughtered lamb to the floor like a child who had finished playing with an old doll. Now, her pin point gaze fell upon the older girl, who still screamed in the corner of the room as she saw her sister's lifeless body crumpled on the floor.

'Do you think I am beautiful?'

'No!', the older girl screamed through gritted teeth at the Woman 'No!'

The Woman's smile faded. A furious grimace took its place. From behind her stained teeth came a low, growling sound growing louder till it was almost deafening. The Woman launched forward towards the older girl, kicking the limp body of her sister to one side across the shattered glass. Her hand shot out from beneath her shawl and she propelled the girl into the air, gripping her head tightly with her black talons so that the girl and the woman were chocolate eye to white eye. She turned with almighty speed and stormed to where the mirror had once been. With the screaming girl clutched in one claw, she stepped through the window into the other world without a returning glance. The moment the Woman and her prey had returned to the other side, a blackness spread across the window creating an opaque space where the mirror once stood. Light returned to the bathroom, fighting back against the shadows. However, the supporting forces were too late.

Later, at five minutes past eleven to be exact, the sisters' mother would return from her shopping trip to discover the horrifying scene that no mother could ever dream of. The mother will place her shopping bags in the kitchen and call out to her younglings. With no answer, she climbed the stairs to their empty bedrooms. Bedrooms that shall remain empty for the rest of her life. The mother called out again, thinking her daughters are playing hide and seek. Smiling, she opens the bathroom door to find the floor covered with shards of mirrored glass. Lying in the centre, the pale body of her youngest child. A child who once filled the house with laughter and love. Now, the child lay outstretched in a sea of her own blood, with a smile forced upon her face. The police would investigate but assume that the older sister had killed her and ran away. The mother insisted that her daughter would never do such a thing, but with no other suspect, the police wouldn't listen. The older sister was never found.

Chapter 1

Worcester

'Thank you for your time Mr and Mrs Bell… I realise we have asked you a lot of questions and you must be tired. I promise you; we will do everything we can to find your daughter. I will put my best men on the case, I assure you. In the meantime, if you think of anything, anything at all, that may be relevant-please don't hesitate to contact my team.' The balding man, who wore an expensive pin-striped suit and fake Rolex watch, rose from his seat behind his desk. On this desk lay a closed silver MacBook, an engraved golden pen set perpendicular to the MacBook, and a golden sign reading 'Detective Johnathon Moore'. On the egotistical walls of his office were pictures of the detective receiving a variety of awards for his service. Detective Moore appeared in the centre of every picture- his chubby, sweaty, red face beaming into the camera. The detective was always proud of these accomplishments, giving a guided tour to any visitors that happened to enter his office.

A sad, withering cactus drooped in a pot on top of an almost empty bookcase containing only a copy of Stephen King's latest novel (a gift from a friend which would remain un-read, gather dust) and the obligatory Bible that was propped up at one end of a shelf. As he stood and extended his right hand towards the couple, the excess stubbled skin around his neck wobbled. 'Thank you for your time, Mr and Mrs Bell,' he repeated again in a formal, yet condescending tone.

The couple remained where they sat for a moment longer staring at the sweaty, purple veined hand hovering mid-air in front of them. Mr Bell's usually neatly combed black hair was now greasy from yesterday's hair gel and his fringe hung low on his ghostly pale forehead. His green eyes appeared sunken in his face as he tried to force them to look up into the detectives eyes. He tried to moisten his lips to say 'Promise me you will find our daughter,' but no words would come. Instead, Mr Bell stood, shook the detective's hand without uttering a word, and left the office. With this, Mrs Bell also rose. Her blonde hair had begun to curl around her neck and her usually bright, blue eyes were now bloodshot red. She did not shake the detective's hand but moved quietly to the door of the office. Once there, she turned to look the detective in the eye. This almost forced the detective back into his seat, as he tried to maintain Mrs Bell's firm stare.

'Find my Lucy,' she whispered. Although her eyes were hard; her voice broke on the name of her child. Before Mrs Bell was overcome with tears once more, she turned and left-leaving his office door open behind her.

Detective Johnathon Moore watched Mrs Bell walk down the row of cubicles towards the exit to the station. His eyes dropped their gaze as they followed Mrs Bell's perfectly curved behind bounce with each stride in her tight running leggings. He thought back to his overweight wife at home, probably sat in front of the telly watching 'Come Dine with Me', with a glass of Coke in one hand and a large bag of Wotsits in the other. His wife and Mrs Bell could be a completely different species. Mrs Bell took one final step before she turned out of view. His tongue ran across his bottom lip, tasting the sugar from the éclair he had eaten moments before the Bells had entered the station.

'That is one lucky husband.' Detective Moore muttered as he closed his office door.

'Excuse me?' came a voice from the corner of his room, startling Detective Moore out of the trance he had found himself in.

Turning, he saw his junior partner, Detective James Bannister, leaning against the rear wall. His oversized, grey M&S suit hung off his thin frame as if it had been worn day in, day out for years without ever being dry cleaned. James ran a hand through his long, mousey brown hair that lifelessly hung over his brow, which revealed his deep, blue eyes that pierced through the dimly lit office straight into Detective Moore's own grey eyes. Although his face concealed any emotion he felt towards Detective's Moore's passing comment; his blazing eyes conveyed his true distaste for the obese man standing before him with his shirt barely concealing the beer gut he possessed. Moore licked his lips once more, wiped sweat from his brow with the back of his hand, and dropped his guilty gaze to the floor. Anywhere to avoid those inquisitive, blue eyes that glared at him across the room.

'Nothing… nothing… I was just… well…' Detective Moore drew his attention to the shining fake Rolex on his wrist. 'Isn't it time you went home Bannister? Your shift has finished hasn't it?' James looked at his own heavily worn Casio digital watch.

'Yes, it finished almost two hours ago. But aren't we going to help find this girl? You know the statistics as well as I do, if we can't find her in under seventy-two hours-'

'That girl will turn up, without using our money and resources to find her.' Detective Moore scratched the side of his stubbled cheek, 'The girl has either panicked and ran away after the babysitter killed the others, or we have a murderer identified. We can put a picture out of her and ask for any information from the public.'

'But what if she needs our help?'

'Who?'

'Lucy. The Bell's daughter. She could still be out there, hurt or worse.'

'Would you stop! I am not going to waste our money on a hunt for one girl. As far as I am concerned, the case is closed. The Bell's placed their trust in a mentally unstable young woman who, for whatever reason, killed the young girls and then herself. The daughter managed to escape, and will turn up in the next few weeks.' The detective picked up his coffee mug, gulped the contents down, and fell into the rouge leather seat behind his desk. The chair gave out a hopeless sigh as his heavy posterior returned once more to its home.

'Sir, I don't think this is right-'

'Well the last time I checked, I hadn't asked for your opinion

Bannister. Look around you, look at all of the awards I have been given over the years. I know what I am doing, and you shouldn't be questioning your senior. Understood?' Moore's chins wobbled again in pride. James' face flushed scarlet and he felt warmth rise up his neck. In his pocket, he clenched his fist and behind his lips grinded his teeth. Eventually, he forced himself to nod. Moore lent back in his chair with a victorious look upon his face. James couldn't stand looked at the pompous toad anymore, turned, and began to exit the office.

'Bannister, before you clock out, can you pour me another cup?' Without waiting for an answer, the mug was pushed into James' hand and the detective had opened his MacBook, the apple glowing in the dimly lit room. The junior detective sighed, gave one last look at the gorilla sitting behind the desk and left the office.

James remembered the excitement and buzz around the office when Detective Moore was given the position. He had a strong reputation for getting things done and that is just what the station had needed. However, as with many who climb the career ladder-once at the top, they become idle. James had watched as power and wealth turned a good detective into a lazy, womanizing, obese oaf, who cared more about where his next doughnut was coming from than finding a missing child. The anger James felt towards the detective as he closed the office door had been replaced with a sense of hopelessness as he knew without Detective Moore's support, Mr and Mrs Bell's case of their missing daughter would go un-investigated and deep-down James knew it wasn't as Detective Moore had speculated. Deep down, James knew there was much more to this case than first met the eye. What James did not know was how this case, and many others like it, would change his life forever.

Chapter 2

Mr Michael Bell and Mrs Sarah Bell walked through the painfully white waiting area of the police headquarters without a word passing between them, without even a momentary glance towards one another. To any onlooker, they could well have been two strangers walking side by side. Both of their faces looked drained of energy, and every step towards the exit seemed to sap a little bit more.

From behind the glass door at the front of the building, they could see the parasitical press competing for prime position to interrogate the parents of the missing girl. Like lionesses hunting for their prey; their eyes lit up and they licked their lips at the site of the distraught married couple shuffling towards the exit.

Photographers raised their cameras to their eyes and immediately bright, white flashes began to assault the building. Each photographer desperate for that one image that would be worth more money than the rest. Reporters stood before camera operators, re-telling the acts that had taken place only hours before. Each News Station with a completely different rendition of what actually happened. Worming fiction into the facts until they are almost unrecognizable but, more importantly, so that the story became more entertaining to entice the mindless viewers at home. Each viewer, no doubt, held their own belief about what had happened that night- taking to social media to argue with others about who was in the right and wrong. Darwin conveyed that in the animal kingdom, only the fittest survived. Humanity is no different, those in power (or worse, believe that they have power), will always prey on the weaker at their most vulnerable times. The powerful only wish to gain more power, and if that meant embellishing the truth about the case regarding Mr and Mrs Bell, then so be it.

Michael put his hand on the cold metal handle that opened the glass door to release the animals waiting on the other side.

'Wait,' Sarah said, putting a hand on his. Her hand felt colder than the steel handle. Taking a deep breath, she looked out at the sea of flashing cameras with a mixture of anger and fear. Like an animal in a zoo, all the press wanted was to make money of her misery. Sarah removed her hand from his, quickly wiped under her nose to ensure the snot was removed and nodded. Michael opened the door and they stepped out into the wild.

'Mr Bell, have there been any developments?'

'Mrs Bell, how do you feel after losing your daughter?'

'Your next-door neighbour commented that she heard shouting beforehand, is that true?'

'What will you say to the parents of the other children? They lost their children because of you?'

'How will this affect your marriage?'

'Do you feel responsible for your daughter's disappearance? Do you think you have failed your daughter as a father?'

Michael's eyes, bloodshot with tears, narrowed as he found the reporter who had asked this last question. The reporter, who stood before a large camera, had bright, blue eyes, slicked back black hair, a weathered face covered with orange makeup and thin red lips. This was a reporter who had outstayed his welcome on the screen and needed a juicy story to re-ignite his career. This was a reporter with nothing to lose and no sympathy for the parents of their missing daughter.

'What did you just say?' Michael muttered with fury flowing through his veins. His face had turned a dark scarlet colour and his fists were now clenched at his sides. Michael could feel the vein throbbing against his temple and his vision became narrowed in, targeted on the bastard in front of him. The reporter, oblivious to the fact he was standing before a savage bull ready to charge, smiled as he thrust the microphone Michael.

'I said, do you feel respons-' Before the reporter could finish his reply, the bull charged at the matador. However, this matador had been in the game too long and was slow to react. What followed next happened in an instant, but would be replayed in slow-motion on News Stations and YouTube across the world-thanks to the many cameras tracing Michael's every move.

Grabbing the news reporter by the front of his neatly buttoned, blue silk shirt with one hand, he rose the other from his side, still clenched, and fired it through the air with all the power Michael could muster until it came into contact with the reporter's tanned, money-making face. There was an audible crack and blood spat from both the reporter's mouth and nose as his face swung to the right, cascading over the pristine white shirt of the reporter next to him. The reporter turned his head towards Michael, eyes filled with shock. He rocked forward on the balls of his feet, before falling back into the sea of press. The press surged over the forgotten reporter, as they now swarmed on Michael-who stood looking with astonishment at his throbbing clenched fist. Michael had never punched a man before, he didn't even like watching the boxing as it was too aggressive, but as he gazed at his weapon he felt better than he had done for the last few hours. From behind him, he could hear voices, but they sounded as if spoken through water.

'Michael!' a woman, presumably his wife, screamed. Then another voice that Michael didn't recognise emerged through the mass of noise and commotion.

'Come with me. Move out of the way, let them through.' A hand gripped onto the back of Michael's shirt and pulled him through the crowd. He turned his head to see the junior detective guiding both him and his wife through the sea of cameras. They parted before him like the sea before Moses, and before long they had reached the edge of the pavement where a taxi awaited them. The detective opened the door to the taxi for Sarah to step into the safety of the vehicle. Next was Michael, who he pushed into the passenger section of the taxi with some force, before the door was quickly slammed close behind him. Before the vehicle began on its route to the nearest hotel, the detective reached through the taxi's open window and gave Sarah a card and looked sincerely into her eyes.

'Mr and Mrs Bell, if you need anything. Anything at all, don't hesitate to contact me on my private number.' With that, he banged on the roof of the taxi and away it sped from the bustling news reporters. Michael looked back through the rear window and watched their hero addressing the crowd.

The news reporter with slicked back black hair, and now a broken nose and most likely a black eye, scrambled to his feet and turned to his cameraman with a grotesque smile on his thin lips.

'Did you get that?'

The cameraman nodded. The reporter's smile grew wider, wrinkles spreading across his tanned, leather face. This was the story he needed to propel him back into the big leagues. For him, the injuries were worth the pain as now his face would be spread across every news station in the area, maybe even becoming a viral sensation. Reaching into his pocket, he pulled out a painkiller and chewed it between his perfectly straight, and fake, white teeth. He ran a sweaty hand through his greased-back hair, and then slid two fingers across his black, trimmed eyebrows. Then, with a nod, the camera man turned the camera back to record.

'Good evening, I do apologise for that interruption to our report. As you will have seen, following a series of questions he refused to answer, Mr Bell savagely attacked me. This occurred moments after Mr and Mrs Bell emerged from their interview with the Chief Detective. The words on everyone's lips here are 'What happened in that meeting with the Chief Detective to create such anger in a man who has just lost his daughter?'. Although we do not know any more details about the case, as the Chief Detective is yet to make a statement; I do believe we have gained an invaluable insight into the true character of Mr Michael Bell. There is more to this case than meets the eye. Does Mr Bell have a more sinister role in all this? I cannot say. But after that vicious outburst... I believe something has Mr Bell rattled. Is it guilt regarding his daughter Lucy who went missing in the early hours of the evening yesterday? Is it the knowledge that if Mr and Mrs Bell had remained at home, five other children would still be alive? Or is Mr Bell hiding a darker secret? Only time will tell. As for Mrs Sarah Bell, she appeared distraught and reserved as she came out of the building- noticeably standing away from her husband of eighteen years... We have just received news from a reliable source that they have not travelled straight to 'The Stalling Hotel' but have gone back to the scene of the crime, their home in Rightdale Street. As you can see behind me, many of the reporters are heading that way now. I will keep you updated on any more details as the case progresses. Back to you Brian and Emily.'

Chapter 3

As soon as Michael was pushed in through the taxi door and the door slammed behind him, the taxi began the ten-minute journey to the hotel the Bells would be staying in that night. The hotel in question, 'The Grand W', was a three-star multi-story, listed building on the outskirts of the main city. Sarah and Michael had frequented the hotel for anniversaries- when they were able to book Michael's mother to babysit Lucy. The building held fond memories for the pair. However, the events of that night would taint those, pushing them into the corners of their mind where eventually the cobwebs would hide them forever.

'Why did you have to do that Michael?' Sarah sighed and put her head against the cold glass of the window. Her head was throbbing and every streetlight the taxi passed sent shooting pains behind her eyes.

'I had to… Did you hear what that pompous prick said?'

'I did but hitting him is only going to make things much worse. You just have to ignore them.'

'That may be easy for you, just to turn a blind eye, but I will not let strangers talk about my family like that.'

The couple sat in silence, watching the morning light slowly reveal the city from it's cover of darkness. Worcester was an unusual city- a mixture of old, beautiful Georgian buildings and hideous modern contraptions that blended into the landscape like a clown at a funeral. Through the centre of the city, the River Severn gloriously snakes to and fro, inviting wildlife into its deceptively hidden strong current.

Sarah found that, as she gazed out of the window at the sunlight reflecting off the golden exterior of the library, any place can be viewed in varied ways depending on mood of the observer. If one was in a joyful mood, Worcester would appear a beautiful city with the luscious green banks surrounding the river. Over which were bridges adorned with locks, each engraved by hopeful lovers who vowed to be each other's till the end of time. However, if one felt as Sarah did, they would observe the cold, steel arms of the bridges linking the two sides of Worcester and think to oneself, 'I wonder how many lonely people jump off that bridge into the freezing, strong current of the river?'

'Stop.' Sarah said to the taxi driver. The driver checked in the rear-view mirror, indicated, and then pulled over to the side of the road. Sarah turned to face her husband, who was also looking out the window with the same expression of hopelessness across his face. 'We need to go back to the house.'

'The police said it's now a crime scene and we aren't allowed back-'

'I heard what they said Michael. Drive to the house'. In the rear-view mirror, the taxi driver's eyes moved between his two passengers, evaluating whether to wait for the husband to respond, or to obey the wife's stern command. His eyes then moved down to the fare calculator that sat over the radio. The prospect of a higher pay-out for these passengers convinced the driver of which path to take, as he checked the side mirror of his black taxi, put the car into first gear and turned the car onto the other side of the road to return back the way they came. Although the driver knew of a quicker route to the Bell's residence; he also knew that his passengers would be too distracted by grief to notice the extra mileage.

'Sarah, they won't let you in. The whole road will be closed off, Michael muttered while maintaining his gaze out of the window. Sarah didn't reply, focusing her attention out of the front window as the taxi driver took a left down a side street.

It didn't take long for the taxi to make it's way across the city to their home on the other side of the river. As the vehicle turned into Asdale Green Road, Sarah saw that her husband's prediction was correct. Michael also recognised this, but decided it wasn't the right time to tell his wife this fact. The car pulled into the curb and stopped. The taxi driver looked down at the fare counter, at the road taped off in front of the car, and then at his passengers.

'Shall I turn back?', the taxi driver asked in a thick Birmingham accent. Sarah looked through the front window, now covered with tiny droplets of rain, trying to clear her mind and decide what to do next. She needed to get into the house, to get something very precious to her, and nothing would stand in her way. She opened the taxi door and stepped out into the cold winter air. Without a word to her husband, she shut the door and looked towards the house that her family had called home for the past ten years.

The house belonging to the Bell family was situated on the right side of a small cul-de-sac road. A traditional semi-detached two storey, orange brick house, currently illuminating the street, as every house light in number 17 had remained on following the occupants leaving the scene. The light emitting from the house revealed the many obstacles that littered the road, preventing Mrs Bell from entering her home.

The road was split into sections of opposing forces. The first of which was the press. The reporters grumbled to each other as they waited for a call from the station that they were going to be back on air. The camera operators were covering their equipment with thin, waterproof covers to protect from the drizzle- also waiting for further instructions from the suits back at the television headquarters. Each camera was lined up outside the yellow police tape that had now been set up from one side of the road to the other.

Behind the yellow police tape were three police cars parked perpendicular to the pavement to block the road. The red and white lights had long since been switched off, but the vehicles remained steadfast to hold back the press. Their owners leant on the hoods of the cars, drinking warm coffee and taunting the freezing News Crew. The detectives had already been in the house, taking evidence and pictures, so they now waited for a call from the top to relieve them of them of their post. The only difference between the police force and the press was that the police force, on the whole, served to protect those from harm. The press desired a story and didn't care who was harmed in the making of it. So long as it gained them top billing on that night's show and provided them with their five minutes of fame, they would continue to exaggerate the details of their story.

Sarah could see, from where she was standing at the side of the taxi, that the police officers shivering inside their uniforms were miserable, their senses perhaps dulled by the relentless drizzle that continued to fall from the sky. This may be easier than Sarah first anticipated. She sniffed the cold, winter morning air, took one look to her right to see that her husband had remained sat in his seat gazing out of the window, and marched purposefully towards her home.

As Sarah approached the press, she considered Steven Spielberg's classic film 'Jaws'. In the film, the rubber shark could sense even a droplet of blood entering the vast ocean from miles away. As Sarah saw the cameras begin to switch on and point in her direction, the news reporters combing their hair and checking their make-up hadn't ran in the drizzle, she thought maybe Spielberg should have made the predator not a shark but the press. They may not be able to smell blood, or bite a chunk out of a boat, but the press could sense a story, smell fear and desperation, and would stop at nothing to get a headline. The first news reporter pounced.

'Mrs Bell, we have heard reports that your husband has assaulted a reporter, do you care to comment?'

'Is the violent assault a sign that your husband has something to hide Mrs Bell?'

Keeping her head down and her eyes forward, she aimed for her front door that still remained open from the detectives searching the house. Although she had lived there for many years; the house before her looked different. Lifeless and cold. She pushed her way between the cameras, through the horrible stench of sweat that circled the cameramen like flies, and bent under the police tape.

Sarah could hear the murmur from behind her as they all pointed their cameras at her, hoping that the wife's temper was as volatile as her husband's. She walked towards the nearest police officer, who currently stood by himself with rain dripping from his police hat, cradling a takeaway cup of warm coffee. He lowered his head to take a sip when his eyes noticed the determined woman walking towards him. The sight of the woman, wearing a sodden white shirt and with her wet hair hanging across her pale face, forced the police officer to halt mid-sip. Their eyes met for a second and Sarah's grimace transformed into a half smile.

'Good evening officer, I suppose you know who I am?' Sarah

didn't want to waste any of her time with pleasantries and knew that the best way to gain access to her house was to be direct with the tired police officer.

'Yes ma'am', the police officer replied. Sarah could see the cogs turning in his mind as he tried to determine the best course of action.

'What was the protocol for this? My shift ends in half an hour, do I really want to cause more hassle for myself?'

'I am ever so sorry, but I think I might have left some possessions in the house that I really need. Would it be alright if I could just pop in to collect them?'

Again, the cogs and wheels were turning. If this were a cartoon, Sarah would see smoke seeping from his ears as his brain began to overheat. Before doubt could enter into the officer's eyes, Sarah took a step closer to the officer- so that her breasts were brushing gently against his chest, under her soaked shirt.

'If Michael saw me now...', she thought, looking deep into the officer's eyes.

'I will only be a second. You could escort me if it's easier officer', she put her hand on his arm and squeezed slightly. There was a moment of silence, then the officer cleared his throat and put his coffee down on the roof of the car.

'I can't see there being a problem with that ma'am. Follow me.', he mumbled and then began walking towards the front door of their house. As Sarah followed the officer in the bright, fluorescent green jacket, she wondered how he might be reprimanded for letting a suspect to a missing child case return to the scene, collect evidence, and then leave. This could well be the end of this officer's career, but Sarah didn't care. She had only one thing on her mind.

The police officer stepped inside of the house first, followed closely by Sarah. He stood on the 'welcome home' door mat and turned with a look of self-importance and authority on his face.

'You can't have long in here Mrs Bell. You and your husband have become quite the stars since your husband hit that reporter. This case went to national news in a few minutes...I shouldn't really be- '

'I know...', muttered Sarah, 'Thank you.' The police officer nodded; his eyes firmly fixed to the beige painted wall behind her as he desperately forced himself not to look down at the woman in front of him. Sarah walked through the entrance hallway, passed the family photos on the walls, towards the stairs. The lights were on but Sarah felt she was walking in a haze of dreams and memories.

Only that morning, Sarah had walked down this hallway towards the door to go to work. She had kissed her husband goodbye, picked the freshly marked schoolbooks off the table with one hand and scooped her car keys out of the key bowl with the other. Sarah remembered opening the front door, turning to shout goodbye up the stairs to Lucy, then shutting the door behind her. That was the last thing she had said to her daughter. Perhaps, if she had waited a moment longer, Lucy would have come running down the stairs and given her a hug before she went. Perhaps, if she had waited a moment longer, Lucy would still be here.

She shook the memory from her head, trying to remain focused on the task in hand. Her left hand gripped the white painted wooden bannister, which now felt cold to her touch. Her legs trembled underneath her, but she forced her right leg onto the first step. A slight moan underfoot as the wood adjusted to it's owner returning, proceeded by another as Sarah dragged her left leg to follow. Slowly, she continued making her way up the stairs with her hand gripping the bannister tighter with each step.

At the top of the stairs, Sarah closed her eyes and took a deep breath. Although she had made the journey many times over their time living at the house; the air felt heavier and forced her to stop with lightheaded-ness. Her mouth was suddenly extremely dry and she could taste a bitterness at the back of her throat. Fear had slithered into her stomach, chasing the butterflies around until she felt sick. Sarah took another deep breath, hoping to force the snake down, but it remained. Climbing and coiling around her heart, tighter and tighter with each breath. Sarah opened her eyes and walked towards the master bedroom. The door had been left open, sending a shiver of panic down her spine.

'Have the police been through my possessions? Have they taken it?'

Forgetting the fear, she raced towards the room. Falling to her knees, Sarah reached under the bed with stretched, searching fingertips. Her fingers made contact. A sigh of relief snuck from her lips as she pulled the box out and put it on the bed mattress. Once opened, Sarah reached in and took out two objects.

One was a brown, leather bound photo album. On the front was a picture of Lucy wrapped in a light pink blanket on the day she was born. Lucy's beautiful, blue eyes shone out of the picture like sparkling sapphires. As Sarah looked down upon her beautiful creation a tear fell through the air, splashing on the leather. She ran a hand over her eyes and put the album to one side on the bed.

The second object was a small golden locket and chain. The cover was adorned with a white gold swirl leading inwards towards a small diamond. Sarah gently pulled the cover and revealed two pictures within. On the right-hand side, a picture of Sarah as a baby in the arms of her mother. On the left-hand side, a picture of Lucy in the arms of Michael who wore the most ridiculous, proud smile on his face. This smile crept onto Sarah's as she sat for a moment longer looking at these two pictures, separated by time but bound with love. The locket had been a gift from Michael for their tenth wedding anniversary. Her husband had never been good at picking gifts for her, but that year he had chosen the perfect one. The locket was never worn, but kept hidden in the box under her bed- with the intention to pass it to her daughter when she got married. A moment which had been taken from Sarah, like many other moments. Sarah wouldn't be there for her daughter's first boyfriend, her daughter's first heartbreak, her daughter's graduation. Sarah felt the weight of the locket in her heart, a weight of guilt that whatever had happened to Lucy should have happened to her instead.

A movement and creak from just outside the bedroom door broke Sarah's trance. Quickly, as she predicted the police officer was getting anxious, she put the lid back on the box and replaced it under the bed, put the locket around her neck and picked up the photo album. Sliding it under her arm, she backed towards the door, past the large mirror on the wall, and emerged back onto the landing- expecting to see the police officer lurking by the stairs. There was no one there. She peered over the bannister and saw the police officer still standing by the door scrolling through Facebook on his phone.

As Sarah began to walk back towards the top of the stairs, something caught her eye. Something that any ordinary person passing by may have missed or overlooked. The door to her daughter's room. It was open. The detectives had probably searched the whole house, including her daughter's room, and in their haste had most likely left the door open. However, as the locket around Sarah's neck gained further weight and pressed into her chest, she couldn't shake the feeling that something wasn't right.

Through the crack in Lucy's door, Sarah could see only darkness. Darkness that seemed to be hiding a presence from her, like something was standing there, watching. Waiting for her to come closer like a spider waiting on her web for an innocent fly to become entangled in it's trap. Every fibre of her being screamed at her to ignore the invitation of the open door. To walk down the stairs to the police officer, where the light of his phone would protect her from the evil within the darkness. But, instead, she walked forward to Lucy's door with her hand outstretched. Her fingertips brushed against the smooth wood and the door swung inwards without a sound. Quickly, intending to startle to spider waiting for her, she reached round the edge of the door frame, found the light switch and flicked it on.

Nothing. The room remained cloaked in darkness.

Crack.

She looked up towards the bulb, then down to the floor, realising the bulb lay broken in several pieces on the floor- a shard crunching under her shoe. As her eyes adjusted Sarah noticed that, scattered amongst the broken glass were fragments of another material. Taking a step forward into the room, she lowered herself to her knees. Carefully, so as not to cut herself, she reached out and picked up a shard of the unknown material. It was a piece of blackened mirror. Although it remained reflective; the shard appeared a burnt, opaque colour. Her eyes flitted across the room to where her daughter's free-standing mirror once stood. Now, an empty wooden frame looked back at her, without a single fragment of mirror in its correct place. The carpet beneath her feet felt sticky. Without looking down, Sarah knew the liquid that had soaked into the carpet.

Although she hadn't been told all of the details; she had learnt that five young girls and the babysitter had been found dead in their daughter's room- throats slit (at least that was what the detective had reported to her). Lucy was not one of them. The bodies belonged to the friends that had been invited for a sleepover with their daughter. The babysitter- a young girl who they had paid to watch the children while they were out- had been downstairs watching the television (this had been confirmed, as the television had remained on when the police arrived at the scene). The babysitter then climbed the stairs to where the children were playing and had slit each throat with a shard of mirrored glass, before enacting the same deed upon herself.

Sarah's eyes moved back to the shard of mirrored glass in her hand. The air had grown unusually cold around her causing the water on her shirt to freeze into her skin. From behind the mirror shard,

Sarah could see her own blue eye gazing back at her. Or was it her own? The colour was the same, but something felt…different. Sarah moved the shard closer to her face then-.

'Mrs Bell! It is time for us to go.' The police officer had begun to climb up the stairs, which groaned to alert their owner of the oncoming threat. Sarah quickly put the piece of mirror into her coat pocket, stood straight up and walked out of the room. Closing the door behind her, the darkness was locked within.

'Did you find what you were looking for?' the police officer asked with a vague sense of curiosity. Sarah guessed that the officer's duty was nearly at an end, and his mind was already looking ahead to what meal his wife had cooked him at home.

'Yes. Yes, I did, thank you.' Sarah plastered a fake smile to her face to show her appreciation of the risk this police officer had taken to let her into an active crime scene. However, just as Sarah's lips stretched to express a smile, the police officer opened the door. There was a flash, blinding Sarah for a moment. It took a few seconds for her senses to return as she stared blankly out into the road with a confused look on her face. Her senses returned, one by one, as with each Sarah realised the sharks had found their dinner. First, the smell of fumes from recently parked cars drifted into her nostrils. Then, she heard the commotion of voices from the pavement at the front of her house. Finally, her vision cleared and she saw the array of cameras pointed directly at her.

'We need to get you out of here Mrs Bell', the police officer said, putting an arm around her waist and gently pushing her out of her house towards the press.

'Excuse me, excuse me. Make a path. Thank you'. The police officer had put his hand gently on Sarah's head to hide her face as he guided her through the press. Once at the taxi, he opened the car door and helped her inside. Sarah looked up at the officer with thankful eyes, to which the man nodded and closed the door. Just as it shut, the Bell's heard the news reporter say '-the question on everybody's lips here are, why is Mrs Shaw smiling less than a day after her daughter has gone missing- at the location of the most horrific murder in recent times. I believe there is more than meets the eye with this case, and I will endeavour to find out the truth.'

By the time Sarah and Michael reached the hotel, the picture of Sarah smiling as she emerged from her house had reached every news station in the country, only sharing the front pages of newspapers with that of her husband punching a news reporter.

Chapter 4

Michael lay on the bed in room 26 of the hotel, listening to the steady hum of the bedside lamp and staring at the white ceiling above him. Many times before had Michael gazed at the pearl white ceiling with a feeling of content, with his beautiful wife lying beside him, but today he only felt lost. He wished he could close his eyes and sleep, even if just for a moment. However, if ever his eyes slowly began to close, a pang of guilt forced them back open.

'Why should he sleep when his daughter was missing?' Michael turned over onto his side and looked at the empty space next to him on the bed.

Sarah was sat at the vanity unit staring at her mobile, willing it to ring. Willing her daughter's sweet voice to be on the other end. But it lay silent on the desk, mocking her for believing that hope would prevail.

'Why did you do it Sarah?'

Sarah blinked, forcing herself out of the daze she had drifted into. 'Do what?'

'Go back to the house. What was so important to get?'

'You wouldn't understand.'

'Wouldn't I?' Agitated, Michael sat up on the bed and glared at his wife on the other side of the room. 'Of course I wouldn't understand. How could I? It's not like I have lost my daughter as well today. It's not like I am feeling everything you are right now. And do you want to know the worst thing? The one person who understands how I feel right now has pushed me away, as if I am responsible.' Sarah ran her finger under the chain around her neck that held the locket and brought the small, white gold face into the light.

'I couldn't leave it. I didn't want it to get lost or- '. Sarah couldn't hold the wave of emotions within any longer. She opened the door and let the tears stream down her crumbling porcelain face. Quickly, she put her hands over her eyes to conceal her face, as if ashamed that she could no longer hold the emotion within. Michael slid himself off the bed and put his hand on her shoulder, unsure of how to comfort her. Knowing that whatever he said wouldn't be able to bring their sweet daughter back into their arms. Sarah shifted her body and pushed her face into Michael's chest, her back rising and falling with each sob. Tears welled up in Michael's eyes and flowed down his cheek onto the back of Sarah's shirt, staining the white shirt like raindrops on a summer's day. They remained embracing each other for the next hour, without moving or losing their grip on each other- holding tightly onto the one lifejacket that will keep them afloat and not lost beneath the waves of despair. Incapsulated in a moment of mourning, together. Only interrupted by the sudden buzzing of Sarah's phone on the wooden surface. Both parents' eyes looked over at the screen to see the contact details and Michael felt his wife's heartbeat quicken with hope- however the phone displayed 'Unknown Caller'.

Sarah reached over, pressed the answer button and brought the phone to her ear.

'Hello?'. Sarah was silent for a moment as she listened to the caller and Michael waited patiently, trying with all his might to push the hope that had formed in his heart down. His eyes met Sarah's, looking for some comfort but found none. Sarah shook her head confirming his suspicions, eliminating the hope in his heart for good.

'Thank you. Yes…thank you. We will see you soon.'

'What is it? Have they found her?' Michael asked, but he already knew the answer.

Without a word, Sarah put the phone on the table, stood up and turned the small television on. On the screen stood a news reporter with a fake tan and a nose still crusted with blood around the nostrils.

'I know that man', Michael said- a slight smile appearing at the corners of his lips when he saw the damage his fist had caused. However, Sarah's eyes shot a disapproving look that wiped the smile from his face. The news reporter held his microphone confidently in one hand, and the wooden handle of an umbrella in the other to protect his fake tan from the onslaught of rain.

'-only a few hours after their daughter Lucy was reported missing, this picture was taken outside of their home....' The footage cut to a picture of Sarah standing inside her house with a large smile plastered on her face. As Sarah looked at the picture of herself, she could feel her blood getting warm with anger. From the corner of her eye, she noticed Michael's fist clench and thought she could almost hear his jaw clenching further with each word out of the news reporter's mouth.

'Although no evidence has been released to the press at this moment; sources tell us the marriage between Mr and Mrs Bell had been fraught with arguments in public. Does this mean there is a secret being kept behind closed doors? We can only speculate what they may be hiding. All we can say for now is that our hopes and prayers are with Lucy and the families of those who have lost on this day. We hope the police find some evidence in the next few hours to help find her. We understand the Bells will be called in for questioning again, following this recent picture of Mrs Bell joyfully retreating from the crime scene. We will bring you further updates as and when we receive them.' Michael switched the television off and silence returned to the room. However now, the silence of mourning was replaced by the silence of anger.

'That bastard', Michael muttered through gritted teeth. Sarah shook her head, trying to keep her emotions in check. The wall had been re-built and she had regained her composure. If Michael had not witnessed her release of emotion minutes before, she would have appeared cold and emotionless.

'It was my fault Michael... A lawyer is on his way to make sure the reporters don't make us say anything we don't want to. He thinks that after that picture, we will become official suspects... I suppose it was only a matter of time.'

'What? They think we did something to our own daughter? They think we hurt our own daughter? And those other girls?'

'There are no other official suspects Michael. Only us. The other suspect is dead.' Michael turned his head to look out of the hotel window to avoid his wife's stare.

'I shouldn't have done it.'

'It is done now. We can't take back what is done.'

'But… they can't honestly believe we… And how did they find out her name? She is a minor, they shouldn't be able to-'

'The reporters interviewed our neighbour from number 4… Miss Caine… she told them everything. About the names, about the arguments we had… everything…' Michael was quiet to this, his gaze fixed to the window.

'Well, you have to admit, looking at the evidence… it doesn't look good Michael.' Sarah's voice sounded almost robotic now, as if her exhausted body couldn't manage to vary her speech pattern to sound appropriately concerned to the current situation. 'I am going to have a shower.' She moved quietly towards the small shower in their room, with only the soft sound of her feet on the carpet, and closed the door behind her. Sarah went into the walk-in shower, turned the dial for the shower and watched as the water streamed out of the head onto the plastic floor. Turning back to the sink on the other side of the room, she put her hands on either side of the basin and closed her eyes. When she opened them, she was met by the same tired eyes looking back at her in the mirror. From the other side of the door, Sarah heard Michael turn the television back on. Not the news this time, but what sounded like a repeat of Top Gear. She slowly unbuttoned her shirt, each button taking an enormous amount of effort to slide back through the hole. After this, she unbuttoned her jeans and slid them down to her ankles. Sarah admired the silky black lingerie she wore underneath and thought about how different last night could have been.

It was true- Michael and Sarah had been struggling with their marriage. With both working seven to five jobs as teachers, they barely saw each other-which only caused strife in their lives. Last night was meant to change all of that. A date night. Time for the two of them to reconnect and ignite the flame that had dimmed to a fluttering ember. After dinner, they would have returned home and drank a lovely bottle of wine. Then, after that…

Sarah slid the silk underwear down her thighs to the pile of jeans on the floor. With one hand, she unclasped her bra and that too dropped to the floor. With a deep breath, she returned to the shower and let the cold water run from her head down her back. With closed eyes, she tilted her head back under the shower head and felt the cold beads chase down her cheeks.

While her eyes were closed, she thought about the days to come. Whether the police would find Lucy. Whether, if the police find Lucy, she will be alive or hurt, or worse. Her mind wandered back to the River Severn, the strong current that pulled any unsuspecting prey beneath its depths. She imagined the flashing police car lights parked on the bank as they search the river-bed. Until one of the nets feel resistance. The police officers begin to pull the net onto land, finding the cold, pale body of her innocent daughter. Whether she would then be taken to court if the police deem her to be guilty of murdering her own child.

She slid one hand through her blonde hair, forcing the horrific thoughts from her mind and stopped. Every hair on her body stood on end and a chill ran down her spine. There was someone in the room. Although Sarah had her eyes closes; she was certain of it. She felt it. There was someone by the sink, watching her. Sarah turned the shower off and stood for a moment- still with her eyes closed, listening. There it was. Low but audible breathing from the other side of the-now steamy-glass partition separating the shower from the bathroom. Sarah took a deep breath. Quickly but carefully, so that she didn't slip on the pool of water at her feet, Sarah moved back into the main bathroom area and forced her eyes open.

No one. No one was there. Only her own reflection staring back at herself once more from the mirror. But she was sure, positive, that there had been someone else in the room. Sarah took the towel from the back of the bathroom door and wiped the water away from her eyes and then wrapped it around her waist. The television could still be heard from the other room, now accompanied by the snoring sound of Michael. *'Tiredness'*, Sarah thought to herself, *'That is all it is. Tiredness.'* She opened the bathroom door and walked back into the main bedroom area of the hotel room, with the full intention to get some sleep before the lawyer arrived.

If, however, Sarah had looked back into the bathroom and had listened intently once more, her suspicions would have been confirmed. From behind the mirrored glass, a young girl was watching through beautifully bright blue eyes. The young girl had her hand on the mirrored glass, willing Sarah to see her. To bring her home. Just as Sarah closed the bathroom door and the automatic light in the room was turned off, a solitary tear ran down the young

girl's cheek and from her mouth she uttered one word.
  'Mother.'

Chapter 5

Five Years Later

Dudley

'So, what do you say sexy?'

The man whom these words emerged from stood at approximately six feet tall, had an unkept beard and his low buttoned chequered shirt- that struggled to withhold the mass of black chest hair underneath- stunk of beer. His teeth possessed a yellowish tinge and a mixture of alcohol and tabaco drifted out of his mouth with this question.

The woman this question was intended for sat with her head on the sticky bar with a glass of straight scotch next to her. Her lifeless, greasy blonde hair hung around her neck and the woman's eyes were firmly closed. Part of her hoped that the man would move on to other prey, but part of her wanted it- wanted the hurt. She sighed, lifted her head off the bar top and drank the last remaining drops of scotch. It burnt slightly as it trickled down her throat and then settled in her stomach. Putting the glass down on the stained wood with a thud, she turned her head to look at the man standing next to her.

'Come on', she muttered as she slid off the chair and then walked towards the male toilets. The man tried to hide his surprised look on his face as he turned to his mates to give them the 'thumbs up'- who were staring with disbelief at this turn of events.

When he made his way into the first cubicle after his conquest, the blonde-haired woman had already slid her jeans and underwear to her ankles and rested her hands upon the back of the cubicle. The man ran his hand through his grubby beard not believing his luck. He walked up behind the woman and pressed his crotch to her rear. The woman felt the bulge in his trousers against her skin and pushed herself backwards further into him. The man undid his belt, unbuttoned his trousers and let them fall down his thick thighs to the floor. The man pushed his erect penis as far as he could into the woman's vagina, expecting a satisfied moan from her. Without reacting, the woman remained in her position and stared at the rear of the cubicle wall, waiting for it to be over so that she could return to the bar. In response, the man wrapped her greasy blonde hair around his right hand and pulled her head back sharply. He moved his hips forwards and backwards to the sound of skin hitting skin.

After a few minutes, the man released a sigh and loosened his grip on the woman's hair. The woman still remained, unmoved. The man pulled his boxers and trousers back up, fastened his belt and staggered out of the cubicle. He took one last look at the arse of the woman still in the cubicle and left the Men's Toilets to tell his mates the details, before returning home to his wife and children.

When she was sure that the man had gone, the woman sighed and stood up. She looked down and saw the man's leavings dripping down her leg. Reaching for the toilet roll, she removed a piece and wiped the remains. Then, pulling her own pants and trousers up, she moved to the water basin and washed her hands. As she looked up into the mirror above the basin, she felt her heart sink, thinking 'What have I become?'

The woman in the mirror had bloodshot, blue eyes and deep, dark bags to accompany them. Far from the bright blue eyes and beautiful, smooth skin the woman known as Sarah possessed only five years ago. These were the attributes of a woman who had lost everything. Lost her daughter, lost her marriage, lost her career, lost her house, lost her life.

Sarah had discovered that a life could be torn apart in five years, and yet her life would still carry on- no matter what she tried to do to end it. Two failed suicides later, along with an excessive amount of drinking and consumption of painkillers, here she remained. Remained to continue carrying her guilt with her like a ruck sack full of reasons God should have chosen her and not her daughter. Looking at her reflection in the mirror, she hated every single part of herself.

Sarah dipped her fingers under the running tap and wiped the cold water under her eyes. She sighed again and walked back out into the bar. The man with the beard had now left, probably thinking his luck would not come again tonight, and the bar was nearly empty- excluding a young couple in the corner of the room. Sarah sat at the bar and tapped her glass again for a refill, refusing to meet the judgmental gaze of the bartender. Instead she watched the young couple, as the young man in a floral red shirt whispered into the ear of the other man with a neatly trimmed beard. With their hands clasped together on the tabletop between their half-drunk beers, Sarah wondered how long they had been together.

'Was this their first date? Did they live together? Had they met the other's parents yet?'

The man with the neatly trimmed beard looked up at Sarah sitting at the bar, more than likely assuming the drunk woman at the bar was being judgmental of their relationship. Sarah smiled and nodded towards him, which relaxed the young man at once. He returned her smile and continued gazing into his love's eyes. She turned back to the bar, where a glass of scotch lay waiting for her to satisfy her craving. Her hands wrapped around the glass and she stared down into the golden liquid inside, thinking about the time she first met Michael.

It had been a cold winter's night in 1978. Michael had picked Sarah up in a rust bucket of a car- a red Ford Escort where only the driver's seat belt fastened into the plug. They had gone to see a film at the cinema, not that Sarah could remember much of the film. She remembered how Michael's hand had slowly moved into her own sweaty one, the tension between them could have been cut with a knife. At the end of the film, just before the lights rose, Sarah had turned to look at Michael to find his lips push against hers with a gentleness that left a soft tingle.

After, they had ended up in a bar not unlike the one Sarah

now found herself in. Although Sarah could not remember every detail about that night; what stood out clearly in her mind is how much they had laughed together. How she had mocked him for having a cocktail while she drank a straight scotch. They had still been on their first drinks, deep in conversation, when the bell rang for last calls. Michael walked Sarah to the taxi and had kissed her deeply before she entered. She had known from that moment that she had found someone special, someone worth trusting with her love. Sarah smiled, reliving her memories and for a moment forgetting that she now sat alone at a bar. But only for a moment. The reality that Michael had left her a year after Lucy had gone missing, and that he was now living in Bewdley with a young girlfriend named Jenny soon returned.

Sarah's grip tightened around the glass of scotch and brought it up to her lips. *Till death do us part, hey?*', she thought to herself, and tipped the glass backwards so that the contents ran down into her stomach to numb the pain. Not any sort of physical pain but pain nonetheless. Reaching into her pocket she withdrew a ten and a five-pound note and slid them across the table to the bartender.

'Keep the change.' Sarah said in a voice that sounded like a cup of gravel had been swallowed. She moved her weight off the stool and walked towards the bar door- trying to keep her vision steady and feet walking in a straight line. Just as she put her hand out to push it open, she turned and looked back towards the bartender.

'Actually,' Sarah reached into her pocket and withdrew a twenty-pound note, 'I'll take the bottle to go.'

Chapter 6

'Mum, wake up.'

Sarah groaned and turned over onto her left side, as she lay on the uncomfortable sofa. She couldn't remember why had fallen to sleep there but knew that she couldn't muster the energy to move to the bed.

'Mum, wake up!' Sarah slowly opened her eyes to the dark living room.

'Follow me.' Sarah looked across the room to corner where the voice had come from. Although the room was nearly pitch black; she could make out the silhouette of a young girl standing by the door to her flat. Squinting her eyes to get a better look, she could only make out her shape and not her facial features. As her eyes adjusted to the dark, more of the young girl became visible. Her heart missed a beat.

'Lucy?' The girl opened the door, letting in a small amount of light that revealed her face. A large, red scar lay across one bruised eye and her lip was slightly swollen from a recent hit, but without any doubt she was Lucy. Sarah's Lucy.

Swinging her legs off the sofa, she stood up, expecting a sudden hangover headache to hit her but felt nothing. In fact, her mind felt clearer than it had been in years. Lucy turned towards the door and walked through without another word.

'Lucy…Lucy, wait!' The mother quickly moved towards the door and followed in her daughter's footsteps through it.

Suddenly, Sarah found herself standing in the shadow of a large, grey house with a rusty, black iron gate in front of her. The house reminded her of the Amityville house, with two large, black framed windows glaring at her and a large, dark red door sat as the mouth in the centre of it's grey face. She looked to her left and to her right, but Lucy was nowhere to be seen. Her fingertips ran over the cold metal of the gate, feeling the rust crumble beneath her touch. It swung open with a creak, inviting Sarah into the neglected garden that lay before the house. Twisted bushes lay around the edge of the garden, with the odd thorned tendril slithering through the dirt towards the gravelled path that led from the gate to the scarlet mouth.

As Sarah looked up at the horrific house before her, something in one of the eyes/windows caught her own. A hand pressed against the glass of the left eye and two bright blue eyes set in a pale face looking down at Sarah. Eyes that a mother would know anywhere. Lucy's mouth was moving, trying to give her mother a message, but the glass refused to let any sound out. Sarah could make out the word 'use' and 'stone'.

'Use the stone? What stone? Use it for what?'.

Sarah stepped forward onto the gravel path. The crunch beneath her first footfall echoed around the silent world around her. Acting like an alarm, the intruder message was sent to the thorned tendril serpents that lay docile in the dirt- igniting a spark within them, giving them life. The serpents began slithering towards Sarah, first slowly as if assessing their prey for weaknesses, then suddenly at a much faster pace- carving a line in the dirt with their thorns. Sarah began to run towards the scarlet door, the gravel path seeming miles longer than first thought. The first of the serpents bit at her left ankle and she winced with pain as the thorn sliced through her skin. Gritting her teeth, Sarah continued towards the door with her hand outstretched for the handle. She could almost touch it. Another serpent cut in front of her and twisted around her ankle, stopping her from taking another step. Sarah reached out as far as she could, her fingers almost on the brass door handle. The serpent twisted up her leg, coiling tighter as Sarah's fingers got closer. Unleashing a desperate howl of pain, she forced her body forward in a desperate attempt to escape the oncoming threat. Hand on the cold brass doorknob, she tried to turn and push the door inwards but it wouldn't move. It wasn't locked, Sarah could feel the click as the doorknob turned; there was something behind the door, stopping it from moving in.

Something warm dropped on her hand. Through the pain of the serpent's thorn, still tightening around her thigh, she felt the warm liquid gain momentum and run off her hand to the floor. Looking down, she noticed that it possessed a dark red colour, similar to the door. However, this wasn't paint. It was blood. As her gaze settled back on the door, Sarah noticed that the same red liquid had started to seep through the cracks of the door and ran down the gravel path.

The realisation came to Sarah too late, and before she could move away the pressure behind the door caused it to explode outwards and shatter into shards of wood. Behind, the wall of squirming, thick blood was unleashed- directed straight at the intruder. Sarah closed her eyes and let out a scream as the blood overflowed, falling like bricks upon her and knocking her unconscious.

The serpents sensed their prey was injured and moved in for the kill. Twisting around her torso and neck, coiling tighter and tighter, feeling the life leave her body with each twist. Then, as if on command, they twisted once more in unison, separating Sarah's head from her body. The head rolled steadily down the river of blood on the gravel path towards the rusty iron gate- coming to a halt on the pavement. The gate swung shut.

Chapter 7

Sarah awoke with a start, rolling sideways off the sofa she had passed out on. She reached out her hand to stop to fall, came into contact with an empty scotch bottle and sent it rolling across the carpeted floor. The headache Sarah was greeted with was as painful as she had expected in her dream, the feeling that an atomic bomb had just detonated in her skull.

'*Or be severed from her body by thorned branches.*' she thought. Without opening her eyes, she struggled to her feet, using the sofa as support, and staggered towards the bathroom. In the cabinet above the sink, Sarah found a bottle of painkillers and withdrew two tablets from the container- adding two more to the collection in her hand for good luck. She put the tablets into her mouth, positioned them between two molars, and bit down- releasing a disgusting bitter taste into her mouth. This was followed this with cold water from the tap, that she also dabbed on her forehead.

Sarah lifted her head up to look at the reflection in the mirror but as she did, something on the surface caught her eye. In the corner of the silver screen there was a messaged etched into the mirror, as if scratched by a knife or sharp nail.

'*Use the stone.*'

Sarah traced the scratched writing with her finger. 'Use the stone.' So many questions spun around Sarah's head simultaneously:

'Who wrote the message?'
'How did the message appear on the mirror?'
'What stone?'

Sarah walked back into the living area she bent down and picked up the empty scotch bottle off the floor, before she tripped over it and ended up with a more severe headache than the one that currently rattled around her mind. As the bottle was placed back on the table, she heard the dark green glass encounter an unknown object that she couldn't make out in the early morning light. Running her hand down the bottle, her skin came into contact with a small, smooth item on the table. She brought the object up to her eyes and her heart nearly stopped.

Lying in the palm of her hand was a small blue stone. It appeared ordinary in appearance, even the shade of blue appeared unremarkable, but Sarah felt a strange sense of power, like an electric current, flowing from her palm to her heart. A feeling that she could not explain, but that felt as if her mind was alive for the very first time. Truly alive, without the constraints of it's human prison. It was as if every atom in her body was suddenly charged and vibrating at an inhuman rate.

'Use the stone... rescue me...mum.' The voice came from behind Sarah, but she recognised the speaker instantaneously. She closed her hand into a fist around the blue stone and spun on her heels to the source of the voice. However, Sarah saw nothing but shadows and darkness. Quickly, she pushed the light switch on the wall, causing the old bulbs to flicker on. Still the corner of the room was empty. Empty apart from a mirror on the wall. A mirror that was not empty.

In the mirror, Sarah saw a face that made her heart swell with love and despair all at once. Her little Lucy. She looked as she had in Sarah's dream only a moment before, but in person the afflictions on her face appeared worse. A smile snuck onto Lucy's face as she watched her mother slowly stagger forward towards the mirror. Tears welled up in both the mother's and daughter's blue eyes. Sarah came within touching distance of the mirror- the window Lucy was imprisoned behind- and she reached out her hand towards her. Lucy's smile faded and she took a step back from her mother's outstretched hand.

'Use the stone mum, please. Please find me.' Lucy whispered, tears flowing freely down her face. 'I love you.'

A thin layer of condensation formed on the mirror clouding the image behind it. Sarah rushed forward and wiped the water away with her hand but was met with only her own reflection. Her daughter was gone.

Sarah wiped the tears from her eyes with the back of her hand and sat back on the sofa where she had slept that night and encountered the vivid, drunken nightmare. 'But it wasn't a nightmare', Sarah thought aloud to herself, 'It was a vision. A message. Lucy needs me.' Sarah looked at the blue stone in her hand once more. Lucy needed her mother, and her mother knew in her heart that she would do anything in her power to get her daughter back into her arms once more. Whatever it took, her Lucy would come home.

Chapter 8

Dudley

Sarah sat at a dusty computer in the almost empty Dudley library, slowly scrolling through the webpages in search of someone that could help her find her daughter. Not knowing what to search for, she resorted to typing in 'supernatural experts' and mindlessly scrolled through the results to no avail. To the left of her sat an elderly man with thick rimmed glasses and a combover-scrolling through information on how to tend to an allotment. To Sarah's right sat a young girl of approximately sixteen with red hair platted in a ponytail down her back. She had a large book in front of her and was scribbling down notes quickly underneath the heading 'Revision' in her notebook. The noise of the man slowly typing the keyboard keys one by one and the scratch of the girl's pen on the pad had ignited the embers of a headache in the centre of Sarah's forehead. It had been several hours since her last drink and she felt the withdrawal symptoms clawing at beneath her skin. Her mind flicked back to the thorned branches in her dream, coiling around her neck-how the thorns dug into her flesh as the branches wound tighter and tighter. She shook her head and pushed the thoughts out of her mind for now, trying to focus on the finger-smudged computer screen.

The keys continued to tap to her left, the pen continued to scratch at the paper to her right. Sarah closed her eyes and tried to block the sounds out and cool the aching in her head.

Suddenly, the sounds stopped. The room fell silent. Sarah peered through the gaps in her fingers and looked at her computer screen. The Google webpage had disappeared, replaced by a Word document with two words repeated over and over.

Find me.

Sarah's finger reached for her mouse and she scrolled down page after page, each with those two words repeated. Turning to her left, where the elderly man had been sat typing, she saw that the seat beside her was empty. The computer screen was turned off and a thick layer of dust covered the surface, as if it had been untouched for years. She turned to her left, expecting to find the same but she was mistaken.

Sat beside her was a young girl with her back towards Sarah, however instead of red, her hair was blonde and the white dress the girl wore was a dulled grey with age. A small tear could be seen in the top left of the dress and a scarlet stain dripped down her back.

'Hello?', Sarah whispered. Before she realised what she was doing, as if a puppeteer was controlling her actions via an invisible string, her hand rose and touched the girl's shoulder. The young girl shuddered under Sarah's touch and recoiled away- hunched over, hiding her face in her hands. Slowly, the young girl turned her head so that Sarah and the girl were face to face.

The girl's once bright, dark hazel eyes shone in the dark, but instead of the white surrounding the chocolate iris, they were surrounded by blackness. Sarah could feel the sadness that lay under the surface of her eyes but her face expressed the contrary. The cut that curved through her cheeks remained open so that Sarah could see through the gap in the skin to the rotting teeth beneath. A mixture of saliva and blood dripped in a steady flow from the corners of her grotesque smile onto the grey dress and trickled down onto the laminated floor of the library.

'Use the ...ssstone...' The words scratched their way up the girl's throat like fingernails on a chalkboard causing her voice to sound hoarse and not her own.

'How? How do I use the stone?', Sarah whispered with her eyes locked into the young girl's. The girl lifted her hand and pointed a pale white finger towards the computer screen. Sarah forced her eyes away from the girl and looked towards the computer screen which glowed in the darkness of the library. The screen had moved from the Word document and now showed a list of websites that related to the mythology of one topic. Mirrors.

'But how do I use the stone? I don't understand-'. Sarah turned back to the young girl with so many questions rolling off her tongue. Suddenly, the lights above her flickered back into life and the student with red hair once again sat to her left. The student looked at Sarah with a slightly worried look on her face.

'Are you okay?'

'Yes, fine. Sorry. I was just thinking. Sorry.'

Sarah turned back to the computer and clicked on the first website in the list, with renewed confidence that she would find answers. Although Sarah couldn't explain what had just happened- whether it had been an withdrawal fuelled dream, or something else; she knew that something wanted her to find her daughter. The webpage opened to a dark background and the information contained was displayed in an old-fashioned scroll. Although the text was badly written, one key word stood out to Sarah throughout the piece. 'Mirror'.

'Are there other worlds to this one? Do portals exist to these other worlds? These questions have been subject to debate for many years. One way in which many researchers believe spirits and demons travel into our world- if such a thing does exist- is through mirrors.

Mirrors have been a source of fascination since the first man watched himself in the reflection of still water. Now, our lives are full of mirrors- whether those in every bathroom or in one's selfie device. Some cultures believe that if someone dies in a room where a mirror is present, the soul is trapped for eternity within it. Some believe that the soul is captured in a photograph, when it is taken.

Others believe that when one looks at oneself in a mirror, they are not looking at a reflection of themselves but rather looking at another form of themselves in an alternate world. Another form that may not human at all, but rather a demon taking the appearance of a human to lure the looker into a false sense of security- waiting to strike and take possession of their body.

It is here, dear reader, that I wish to share my own personal story. There is a hotel near the city in which I live that has a reputation for being 'haunted'. Since being built in the 16th century, the hotel had witnessed a total of one hundred and twenty-three murders, sixty-two rapes and fifty-six suicides. The hotel had burnt down and been rebuilt three times, each in the exact design of the original. Many believe the spirits of these lost souls remain in the building, roaming the halls in search for peace or to cause havoc on the unsuspecting guests.

As a serious supernatural investigator, when the invitation to stay at the hotel arrived in the post, I could not resist the opportunity to explore a place with so much dark history. When I arrived, the receptionist gave me a room key to room 254 and I took my luggage up to my room on the second floor. Immediately, I felt the dark energy flowing through my body when I stepped foot into the room that would be my prison cell for the night.

At precisely 1:23am, I was awoken from my slumber by a low moaning sound coming from the far side of my room. I assumed the walls were thin and a passionate couple resided in the hotel room next to mine. So, I rolled over and tried to get back to sleep. Until the moaning became louder and was followed by a dull tapping. I wiped my eyes, sat up in my bed, and looked towards the corner of the room where the noise was originating from. There, stood in the corner was a large, black framed, free-standing mirror. Within the frame stood a man in a long black coat and a top hat lying on a slight tilt on his head. I quickly moved to the lamp on the side table and turned it on. However, when I turned my attention back to the mirror, the man had disappeared.

This event led to my investigation into the mythology of mirrors and I will continue my research till I discover an answer into whether this experience was merely a vivid dream or reality.

If you have any information, or have experienced such things yourself, you can contact me via my phone number or email.

Nick Sharp.

12th November 2001.

As Sarah read this passage, her mind flicked back to her own experience. Of how her daughter had appeared and taken her through the door to the house in the dream. However, that had not involved a mirror. So how did mirrors relate to finding her daughter?

Sarah began to drum her fingers on the computer table (a habit that Michael had always hated) and then stopped when an idea floated into her head and her hand moved to the locket necklace around her neck. There had been a mirror the night Lucy was taken from her.

That night Sarah had returned to their family home to retrieve the photo album that currently sat on her bedside table and the necklace that she had not taken off since then. As she had made her way back downstairs, Lucy's bedroom door had been open slightly. She had peered inside to find shards of mirror scattered on the floor.

At the time, Sarah had thought nothing about it but now, as she read through Nick Sharp's supernatural encounter, she realised that there was a connection. Sarah's mind began to whir, thinking of all the possibilities. Perhaps Lucy had not been kidnapped by someone from this world, nor had she run off as Detective Moore had declared. Perhaps something from another world had taken her- this thing that Nick Sharp had seen in the mirror, with the top hat- through the mirror. It sounded insane as Sarah considered this idea, but no matter how ridiculous, she knew in her heart it was the truth. There was no other option other than the one that Sarah refused to believe, that her daughter was lying at the bottom of the River Severn.

The student beside her put her pen down on the pad she had been scribbling notes on and made her way to the Women's toilets. While she was gone, Sarah reached over and removed a piece of paper from the notepad. She quickly scribbled down the phone number of Nick Sharp, turned off her computer and made her way from the library back to her flat. In the reflection of the computer screen, the little girl with blonde hair and hazel eyes watched her leave with a carved smile upon her face.

Chapter 9

Hello?'

'Good Morning, is this Mr Nick Sharp?'

'Who's asking?'

'Hello Mr Sharp, my name is Sarah. Sarah Bell. I was calling to see… to ask… you see I saw…'

'If you could hurry up, I have an appointment in five minutes.'

'Oh… yes of course. You see, I came across your webpage today and it stated that you investigate the unusual… supernatural things.'

' *Supernatural things'*. Yes, I do Miss Bell. I am a paranormal investigator that explores matters that cannot be explained by modern science. How may I help you?'

'I need your help because… well.. you see my daughter went missing five years ago'. She waited for the customary 'I am so sorry' but heard none. She continued, 'The police concluded that she may have been kidnapped or ran away but… I know this isn't true.'

'Miss Bell, I don't investigate such things. As I have just explained, I investigate matters of the supernatural and paranormal. Perhaps you would be better visiting a clairvoyant or buying a Ouija board.'

'But this is. Or I think it is. I went into her room after she had gone… after she had been taken and there were fragments of her mirror scattered on the floor. And then I-'

'Wait.' Sarah could hear Nick on the other end of the phone clicking a pen and dragging a pad of paper over a table towards himself, 'Carry on please. In as much detail as you can.'

The sudden change in character of Nick Sharp had shaken Sarah-something had peaked his interest.

'Do you think that-'

'I can't be sure Miss Bell. However, I have learnt from my past experiences that whenever a broken mirror is concerned in a story of the supernatural, it requires my upmost attention. So, please, give me as much information as you can so that I can create a picture for myself in my mind.'

'Well… when I went into her room, there were fragments of the mirror over the floor and I felt… I suppose I didn't feel alone in the room. You know that feeling you get, as if someone is looking over your shoulder?'

'Yes. Carry on.'

'Then, a few nights ago I-'

'Why did you go into your daughter's bedroom? I said to provide me with all of the details.'

'I don't see how that helps…'

'Miss Bell, if you want my help then do as I say. Considering you rang me on this number, I presume you do require my help, so answer my question. In as much detail as you can…Please.'

'Okay…I am sorry… I went into Lucy's bedroom because the door was left open. There seemed to be something calling from within, tempting me to look into the room. Not literally, but like a voice in my head. Obviously, when I opened the door and looked inside it was empty.'

'Obviously.'

'There were no other instances like this for the next few years. I had completely forgotten about this incident until this morning. Only, a few nights ago, Lucy came to me in my dreams, asking me to find her. To rescue her. She said to use the stone. I would have passed this dream off as just that, a dream… however when I woke up, I found a small blue stone on the table side. It feels… I don't know how to explain it. It feels powerful, like there is an electricity contained within it.'

'And what happened in the dream?'

'I followed Lucy through a door in my flat. On the other side, I found myself standing in front of a large house. Lucy was looking down from a window, asking for me to help her. I approached the house by following the front path when-'

'I have heard enough.' Sarah's heart sank. He must not believe her case to be supernatural at all, merely the wonderings and dreams of a desperate, alcoholic mother of a kidnapped daughter. All she had done was waste his time. 'Come to my home office next Wednesday, that will give me enough time to gather all the information I need to fully understand the situation. I live at 23 Sail

Lane in Stratford-upon-Avon. You will recognise my house by the red door. Bring the stone. Although it may be too soon to say conclusively; that stone may be the key to it all. Till then, Miss Bell.'

With that, Nick Sharp hung up the phone, leaving Sarah standing with her own mobile pressed to her face in disbelief. Before the address left her mind, she wrote the it on the back of a business card that had been discarded on the side table.

The stone. 'The stone may be the key to it all.' That is what he said. The key to getting her daughter back. With that thought filling her mind, Sarah's heart fluttered and she felt a sudden warmth flow through her body that she had not experienced since Lucy went missing. Hope has the power to make even the darkest days appear bright. However, most commonly, hope merely creates a false sense of positivity to give the person one moment of good before the darkness of despair descends once more to suffocate out any life that remained. But Sarah didn't care, as for that one moment of good, Sarah believed with all her heart that she was getting her Lucy back.

Chapter 10

Bewdley

The sun flooded through the semi-opened blinds into the large bedroom of Michael Bell's apartment and danced over the fresh, white bed cover that lay across the king-sized bed that currently held two bodies lying close together in the centre. The one body was that of a thirty-year-old black-haired woman, who lay with her back to Michael behind her. The sunlight kissed her pale cheeks and waltzed over her lips to gently wake her from her pleasant dream of the possible futures for her and her partner. Letting out a deep sigh, she opened one of her eyes to look at the alarm clock that faced her on the side-table. It read six o'clock, meaning the alarm wouldn't go off for another fifteen minutes. The woman gently shifted her body under the quilt cover and pushed slightly backwards into the crotch of the man lying behind her. This action was responded to by Michael's lips gently kissing the back of her neck.

'Good morning.' Michael whispered into the ear of the woman and he lay his face against her bare back. The woman shifted her body again, repeating the same action.

'You can't do that my dear,' Michael said between kisses upon her pale skin 'when you know we have to get up in about fifteen minutes.' The woman pushed herself back into Michael again and felt the bulge against her upper thigh.

'Jenny… stop.' Michael smiled and gently turned her body to face him. Jenny smiled and gazed deeply into Michael's green eyes. The eyes of the man she loved with all her heart. Michael looked back into Jenny's eyes, also with love, but a part of him knew she would never be the person he loved with all of his heart. His heart belonged to someone who was taken from him five years ago. Jenny knew these scars still ran deep within Michael and knew that, no matter how happy their lives may be in the coming years, he would always feel a slight amount of guilt for that happiness. However, for the year that Michael and Jenny had been dating, Michael had been the happiest he could under the circumstances.

Michael leaned forward and he gently kissed her lips as the sunlight had done, only this kiss sent a warm sensation through both their bodies. Michael broke away slightly, but Jenny pushed her lips harder onto his and shifted her body so that she was lying on top of him. She moved her hips so that their bodies were perfectly aligned then- the alarm clock rang loudly on the table. Jenny laughed and rolled herself off Michael to her side of the bed and put her hands over her face in frustration. Michael swung his legs from under the bed covers and put his feet on the wooden floor.

'I guess that means it is time for work.' He smiled and slid his feet into his slippers. While he had his back to Jenny, she had turned the alarm off and also put her slippers on that lay on the floor her side of the bed. She let out a moan, stood up and made her way to the bathroom. Michael watched as she exited the room, and then began his usual morning procedure.

Every morning, Michael selected which suit, shirt and tie he would be wearing for the day of work ahead and hung them up on the back of the door. He then shaved and, when Jenny was finished in the shower, he went into the bathroom. Once showered and dressed, he met Jenny in the kitchen (which overlooked the sitting room in their two-bedroom modern house, which they rented) and they ate their breakfast together whilst listening to the radio. At half past seven, they left their house and drove to the local primary school where they both taught. It was at this primary school that Michael and Jenny met each other.

Three years after the disappearance of their daughter, Michael and Sarah filed for divorce. The loss of Lucy became a void between them that only grew with each passing day without her daughter, and without any answer to where she was, or what happened to her. Michael had suggested marriage counselling, attempting to save the last part of his family that remained. However, Sarah had become distant and spent her days frequenting the local bar to silence her guilty thoughts. Michael was determined to do whatever he could to support his wife, helping out where he could with her work and at home. That was until one day Sarah didn't come home. Michael tried calling her mobile, to no reply. Eventually, after checking all other options, he visited his wife's bar to discover from the bartender that his wife had left drunk in the arms of a young man. Michael couldn't believe that Sarah would do this, after everything he had done to support her, but the bartender commented that there was only one reason she had left with the man. This was the final straw that broke Michael's heart. He had packed his clothes and left that night, staying with a friend nearby. The part that crushed Michael the most, was that Sarah hadn't apologised for her actions. When Michael told her he wanted a divorce, she merely shrugged.

Within that year, Michael came to the decision to leave Worcester, and the negative memories associated with it, behind him and he moved to Bewdley in search for a new life. He found a job at the local primary school to teach Year Five and met Jenny Doone, who taught in Year Two at the same school. The chemistry between them was immediate and, after a drunken Christmas party, the two decided to date. A trial at first, as Michael confessed he wasn't sure he was ready for commitment. Thankfully, Jenny was the perfect person for him and had arrived into Michael's life at the perfect moment, enabling him to create a new life for himself. He had not spoken to Sarah in almost a year at this point, not that he hadn't attempted to make contact with her. No matter how much hurt she had caused him, a little part of Michael would always love her. He had tried to call her every week after moving out of their family home, but Sarah refused all. He presumed Sarah had moved on with her life, as he had done with Jenny.

Until Michael and Jenny arrived in their car at the primary school that day and found Sarah standing at the school gates tapping her foot, with a concerned and impatient look on her face.

Michael pulled into his designated space in the staff carpark and switched off the ignition.

'What is she doing here?' Jenny asked. Michael sensed an undertone of jealousy in her voice, that he knew would never leave.

'I don't know. I am sure it's nothing.', but Michael knew it wasn't nothing. The look in his ex-wife's eyes told him it was news about her daughter. He hoped that it wasn't news that they had found her body, even though he still expected to receive that phone call every day, every time his mobile rang. 'I will see you inside.'

Jenny opened the car door, stepped out with her school bag across one shoulder and gave Sarah a judgmental look from shoes to hair. When their eyes met, Jenny raised her eyebrow slightly, as if saying 'He's mine now'. Turning on the spot, she strode into the reception area of the school as Michael opened his door and got out of the car.

'Hi Michael.' Sarah's voice carried across the carpark like a leaf in the breeze. Michael had not heard his ex-wife's voice in so long, but even now he could tell the amount of alcohol she had consumed from the hoarse way she had spoken those two words. She turned her back to him to look at the houses that lined the school drive, signalling for Michael to join her. Michael considered his options- to either join Sarah or to leave her on the pavement, going into the school after his partner.

He locked the car and walked towards Sarah, his heart pounding faster with each step. It reminded him of a game the children played at lunchtime, 'What's the time Mister Wolf?', where the children crept closer to the wolf while one child had their back turned. The wolf could turn around at any moment, but still the children crept forward-growing more excited as they got closer. Michael reached the wolf and stood behind her silently for a moment, trying to form words in his dry mouth.

'Why are you here Sarah?' he managed to force out of his mouth in almost a whisper. Sarah turned back to Michael with tears in her tired eyes.

'I saw her.'

These words sent a chill down Michael's spine.

'What… How…She's…'

'She came to me last night. To my flat. I saw her in my dream.' Michael's heart sank. He hated himself for raising his hopes, but he hated his ex-wife more for raising them.

'A dream… You saw her in a dream?'

'Yes but then- '.

'No... No Sarah. I can't...' Michael struggled to find the words, his blood had turned from cold to boiling and he felt the heat rising in his face. 'She is gone Sarah. Gone! She visits my dreams too but that is all they are. Dreams.'

'No, but... listen... She wrote on my mirror. She gave me a message and left this...' Sarah fumbled desperately in her pocked for the small blue stone.

'Sarah, I can smell the scotch on your breath from here. She is gone. I suggest you move on. She isn't coming back.' Although these words were spoken by Michael in a definite, decisive tone; they still destroyed him inside to hear aloud from his own lips. He wished the words weren't true, and prayed every night for Lucy's safe return to them, but he knew deep down that his daughter was never coming back. Michael turned away from Sarah and wiped a tear away from his eye. 'I suggest that you go. I have work to prepare for and the children will be arriving soon.'

'Wait. Take this.' Sarah removed a business card from her pocket. 'I thought you might not believe me... but take this. Please. It has the details on if you change your mind'.

Michael snatched the card from her hand, turned and moved purposefully towards the school reception and fought every impulse to look back at Sarah-who stood alone on the pavement. He reached the entrance door, pulled it open and walked inside, leaving the door to swing close behind him.

Sarah looked down at the blue stone in her hand, then at the school building.

He doesn't believe me... why should he? If I hadn't seen it for myself, I wouldn't believe it.', she thought and placed the stone safely back into her pocket. *'If Michael won't help me, I will have to find somebody who can.'.* She took one last look at the school building, hoping Michael would appear from the door and come back to her, but the door remained closed. So, she took a deep breath and walked down the road to her car. Little did she know, the next time Sarah saw Michael would be her last.

Chapter 11

Stratford-Upon-Avon

Droplets of rain splashed off the matt black, metal letter box fastened to a small white picket fence that belonged to the house next door to the Sharp residence. The neighbouring house belonged to a small man who possessed more hair in the thick grey moustache under his small nose than in the few whispers of grey strands he called hair on his head. His name was Nigel Renter. Nick Sharp despised Nigel Renter. Not for any particular reason, Nigel always said 'Good morning' or 'Good evening' if he saw Nick outside his house or in the town of Stratford-upon-Avon, and he always moved Nick's black bin back onto his drive after the bin men had come to collect his rubbish. However, regardless of these good deeds, every time Nick saw Nigel his stomach clenched and he could feel his blood run hot. Through gritted teeth he would reply to Nigel's pleasantries and, as soon as he had moved out of ear shot, Nick would mutter some profanity under his breath. Nick would never dream of saying such things to his neighbour's face, as that was the cowardly man Nick had become as he aged, but he would say them none the less for his own satisfaction.

At that moment, Nick was peering out of the window of his

own home, with his head pressed against the glass, listening to the rain ping on the metal casing of the letterbox. The story that the woman had detailed on the other end of the phone were swirling around in his mind, encased in barbed wire so that every time a word came into contact with another, a shot of pain caused him to wince. The pain killers he had taken minutes after hanging up the phone should take action any moment now, allowing Nick to think about the situation he suddenly found himself in. However, for the moment, Nick had to resort to pressing his head against the cold glass.

Movement on the street outside caught Nick's eye. A short man with a grey moustache was sloshing down the pavement wearing a light mustard suit (which he always wore when venturing into the town). He was holding a black umbrella in his right hand and a newspaper under his left. Nigel came to his own small white wooden gate in his front garden and opened it, about to follow the gravel path up to his cottage. Before he stepped onto his property he stopped, turned his attention to Nick in the window. He made a cup gesture lifting it to his mouth and mouthed the words 'Had a few too many?' with his detestable smiling lips under his caterpillar moustache. Nigel then lifted his left hand to bid Nick a good day and walked past Nick's line of view and into his house.

'Tosser.' Nick mumbled and pressed his head further onto the glass. He remained in this position for about five minutes. A soothing coolness flooded over him and his headache began to subside- even though Nick knew that the headache remained hidden in the recesses of his mind and would explode with more force later that day.

'Now to business.' Nick thought and moved back into the kitchen of his house where his laptop was already fired up, ready to investigate further into the case that Nick believed could be the making of his career. More than that, it could give his life purpose. This could be the proof he had been looking for, the proof he needed to put his middle finger up to all those who ridiculed him.

Nick's house was of the same model as Nigel's- the same white wooden fence outlining a small portion of front garden, the same light blue painted window frames and the same narrow gravel path that led to his red door (Nigel had a dark blue door). The front garden was over-grown and weeds peered out of the gravel path at any visitors that may be wandering towards the door- even though

Nick had not welcomed visitors into his house for a very long time.

Inside the small, detached bungalow was a series of unremarkable rooms- a small living room, kitchen, bathroom and bedroom containing a single bed. Nick had never been a man who required any company other than his own to keep himself occupied. That isn't to say he wasn't attracted to other people, of course he was and he watched porn like any other person in this world, but to share a residence or even a bed with one was out of the question for him. Not that most people would find Nick attractive to look at. Nick had a shaved head (shaved by himself using a razor ordered online, ensuring that he did not need to interact with any over familiar, conversationalist hairdressers) and the dark brown hair stubs sat on his head like a shower cap. To onlookers on the street, they would see an overweight man in his forties with a double chin, a bright red face and the beginnings of a monobrow.

The truth was that Nick was in fact thirty-two and, although overweight, his bright green eyes conveyed that his mind was much faster than his body, and was his true asset. Since realising at a young age that he would never be a professional football player, he had spent his spare time in the library- reading any book that he felt might put him on a higher pedestal than those around him. Nick had spent many weekends sitting in the library during his youth, with one hand in an extra-large bag of crisps, and the other skimming through a book. However, the invention of the internet had removed even that interaction with people, and now he spent his evenings scrolling the internet- still with a bag of crisps close to hand.

Before his body had settled into the kitchen chair, his fingers were frantically typing at the keyboard. The first thing he typed was 'missing children in my area'. He began scrolling down the list of websites but before he reached the bottom of the page, he clicked back onto the search box and typed in 'missing children, mirrors'. Nick's interest lay not in Miss Bell's individual case, but rather the circumstances that surrounded it.

The new search uploaded it's results onto his MacBook in seconds, and his beady eyes were scanning the brief descriptions under each heading. A bead of sweat trickled down the side of his face. Without taking his eyes from the screen, he wiped the bead away with one small, chubby hand. His eyes rested on the third result, under the heading 'The mystery of mirrors'. The description underneath read- 'A series of mysterious cases of disappearances, each linked by one thing. A broken mirror'.

Nick tapped the cursor over the hyperlink and the white search page dissolved into a webpage with a light blue background. The site was arranged similar to his blog, with a long passage of writing down the centre of the page, divided on occasion by a small picture. Nick ran his tongue over his lips and tasted the salty sweat that glistened under his nose and above his upper lip.

Moving quickly, his eyes darted from side to side as he read the writing on the screen. To others, he might have appeared to be skim reading it, but this was certainly not the case for Nick. He was able to read, understand and retain every word that he read without re-reading any sentences- a skill he learnt as a child. The only phrase his eyes rested on, even if for only a second longer, was 'small blue stone'. Nick's mind continued to whir inside his head, the headache had been pushed aside and replaced with an overwhelming feeling of excitement coursing through his blood.

When Nick's eyes reached the bottom of the page, he let out a deep sigh, which suggested he had held his breath for the entirety of reading the passage of writing. He moved his bodyweight back in his chair, which released a small sigh itself as the air was pushed out of the cushion he was sitting on. Once more, he ran the back of his hand over his brow to stop the sweat from running into his eyes. A smile had grown on his face, like a boy coming down the stairs at Christmas to find a series of presents under the tree. Nick had never been a fan for Christmas, having two older siblings who quashed any belief of Santa Claus at a very early age had ruined the festivities somewhat for him. Now he lived alone, with no living family who he kept in touch with, Christmas had become the same as every other day. However, if a transcript from this webpage had been resting under the Christmas tree, Nick's opinion of the season may well have been different entirely.

Moving his large head from side to side, he heard a crack in his neck. He transferred all of his weight onto his tiny legs and moved towards the door with surprising speed. As he passed the side table, he picked up his wallet and checked the contents for his library card. He found it hidden behind a subway loyalty card and an old cinema ticket. Although Nick preferred to search online, he knew that the information he was in search of would be hidden away within old, long forgotten, books.

Sliding his coat over the top of his shirt, he opened the

front door and stepped foot onto the paved slab. As he turned and slid the key quickly into the lock, a voice emerged to the right of him.

'Off out are we?' It was Nigel.

'Yes, I am Nigel.' For once Nick spoke these words with a genuine smile on his face, 'I am indeed. Have a nice day!'

Chapter 12

Raising her enclosed fist up to her eyeline, Sarah rested her knuckles on the red door. She looked at her hand, willing it to knock on the door, but it refused to move. She took a deep breath, held it for a moment, and then released. Just as Sarah felt her knuckles come into contact with the wooden door, it swung open and revealed a large man standing in the doorway.

It was obvious to Sarah that Nick had recently shaved his face as there remained a small red dot of blood on the underneath of his double-chin where the shaver had caught. He wore a black shirt, black trousers and a crimson tie that stood out brightly against the rest of his attire.

'Come this way Miss Bell.' he gasped as he moved his body to one side so that Sarah could squeeze past him into his house. It only occurred to Sarah then, that she was walking alone into a stranger's house without letting anyone know where she was or who she was with (other than her ex-husband but his reaction suggested he would rather her disappear than interfere with his 'perfect' new life again). In the corner of her vision, she saw the thin slit of natural light grow thinner and then disappear entirely as Nick pushed the door shut. Pushing the rising fear that had developed in her stomach back down, Sarah moved into the only room that had a light shining out of it- the kitchen.

As Sarah reached the doorway to the kitchen, she saw a large wooden table to one side of the room with a pile of books and papers resting upon the top. To the right of this was a kitchen work surface- equipped with microwave, toaster, kettle, and other similar items.

However, what caught her eye t and sent shivers up her spine was solitarily standing in front of the oven. A large free-standing mirror. Sarah moved towards it instinctively, her hand outstretched. She half expected Nick, who had followed her into the room, to suddenly shout at her not to touch it. But he did not. Sarah's fingers met the cold metal that was woven in an ornate pattern around the rim of the mirror. At her touch the top of the mirror swung back slightly and released a high-pitched squeak.

In the reflection, Nick moved his enormous mass into a chair at the table and gestured to the other with his large hand. Sarah turned her back to the mirror and walked towards the chair. As she did so, she noticed Nick's eyes move past her, looking at the mirror with a shade of cautiousness behind his pupils. Sarah resisted the urge to look back at the mirror, resting her own weight in the chair that had been chosen for her. Nick's eyes moved quickly from the mirror to her's, and a gentle smile replaced the anxious line that his lips had formed when Sarah turned her back on the mirror.

'Allow me to formally introduce myself Miss Bell. My name is Nick Sharp, the man you spoke to on the phone. But of course, you knew that already.' He wiped the nervous sweat that had formed on his upper lip away with the side of his hand and continued to speak, never taking his eyes from Sarah's. 'I have to say Sarah, may I call you Sarah?' Sarah nodded without hesitation, so as to not break Nick's train of thought. She couldn't explain how, but she knew deep in her heart that what he was about to say would change her life forever.

'Your phone call, Sarah, got me very excited. No, not excited- that is the wrong word for such a circumstance that you find yourself in. For which I am very sorry, by the way. Very sorry... Intrigued, that is the word. Intrigued to hear what you had to say.' Nick leant forward, the table between them shifting slightly under his weight. 'You see, I have been investigating the supernatural, the paranormal, the things that cannot yet be explained, for over fifteen years now. However, I am yet to find anything that can be classed as... well as evidence I suppose. Not that I haven't investigated many cases mind you. This will be my 32nd case, but as you can imagine many of my cases led to either a prank, an old creaky house, or in one instance a cat stuck in the attic. When I first heard you recount your tale, I began to think that, without intending any offence, that you may be delusional. Creating a fantasy where your daughter is still alive, to give yourself some comfort. It is common, when someone loses a loved one, that they create an imaginary world for themselves to help them cope with the loss.' Sarah's face turned a dark shade of red at this remark and she opened her mouth to condemn such insinuations but was halted by Nick raising one chubby finger.

'However, then you mentioned something that forced me to delve back into my memories, back to something I had read many years before, whilst researching another case. The blue stone. You have brought it haven't you?'

Sarah moved her hand to withdraw it from her jeans pocket. As her hand moved closer to the stone, a buzz of electricity seemed to implant itself in her ear getting louder as her fingers got closer-.

'Not yet.' Nick almost barked this command and forced Sarah to move her hand back from the stone quickly. Seeming to shock himself with the forcefulness of this order, he raised his hand as if to apologise.

'Not yet.' he repeated in a lower tone of voice, 'So long as I know you have it, that is enough. Like 'The One Ring' in Tolkien's stories, I fear if I see it, I will become it's slave.' With that he released a little chuckle, wiped his sweaty upper lip again and found his train of thought once more. 'Many years ago, I read a myth that seemed to revolve around that blue stone and the object that stands ominously behind you.' Sarah felt the urge to stare at the mirror once more and this time could not resist, turning her head slightly to look at it from the corner of her eye- only for a few seconds before returning her attention to Nick. The corners of Nick's lips rose slightly as if he also knew all too well the urge to look into the mirror's beckoning reflective surface. He put his hands on the laptop screen and turned the device round for Sarah to see. On it, there was a PowerPoint presentation of sorts, with pictures on each slide.

'Would you like a glass of water before I begin?' Sarah shook her head without hesitation, her eyes were transfixed on the first image on the laptop and she wanted Nick to begin his 'presentation' as soon as possible. Shown on the screen was a rough sketch of a woman, or a figure that resembled a woman. The figure's fringe stuck to her forehead, whilst the rest hung lifelessly from her head. The eyes had no iris, only black, staring out from the laptop screen like two pieces of coal that had fallen into the snow after a snowman had melted. Her nose, almost like that of a bird's beak, pointed out of the screen above the horrific mouth. The artist, whomever it may have been, had drawn the lips aggressively leaving multiple strokes of the pencil on the paper curving up the woman's cheeks. Had the drawing not been sketched with such anger, the smile almost looked amusing, stretched from ear to ear like a clown's. Sarah's eyes drifted from the mouth down to the woman's neck, around which she wore a pendant with a small stone held into place with a clasp.

'Is that-?' Sarah muttered; her lips dry with fear. Nick nodded. He allowed Sarah to stare into the figure's cold, opaque eyes for a moment longer, interested to observe her reaction. His own reaction had been similar and even now Nick avoided looking at the horrific picture in fear that as he looked into those black eyes, the drawing would blink.

'She is known by many names. Abyzou, Kuchisake-onna, Baby Blue, Bloody Mary-', Sarah involuntarily took in a sharp breath at this name causing Nick to stop. Keeping her eyes firmly on the picture, her mind wandered back to when she was a child. To a horrifying night that she was a distant memory, but with that memory came so many dreadful nightmares. When Sarah was a child, her sister attempted to summon the ghost known as Bloody Mary into their bedroom, late one Halloween evening when their parents had gone to sleep. They followed 'The Rules', standing before the mirror holding a candle and saying her name three times. On the third, the candle blew out and both sisters had screamed. Sarah had long suspected that her sister had blown the candle out to scare her. But it didn't stop the feeling that, when the candle had extinguished, something had been watching them from within the darkness. Perhaps if their parents hadn't rushed into the room and turned on the light...

'Is everything alright Mrs Shaw?' Sarah regained control of herself, pushing these memories from her mind and burying them once more. She nodded for Nick to continue.

'Good. As we don't have much time.' Nick announced this with a mixture of urgency and authority. Sarah felt that the man sitting before her wasn't well versed in polite etiquette and very rarely had a guest in his house. He coughed, wiped the sweat from under his nose with a finger, and continued with his presentation.

'The most common name this woman is known by is 'The Smiling Woman'. I assume I don't need to explain to you how she gained such a name? The Smiling Woman has as many origin stories as she does names- depending on where you are in the world. From my extensive research, I have deduced which tale I believe to be the most credible. That being said, I do believe in every story, there is an element of truth. A thread that could be linked to another, and another. I have not had time to follow this thread, however the story that began all others… it is not a story for the fain of heart.' Nick watched the woman before him, waiting to see if she showed any ounce of fear, but the woman remained focused on him. He moved the laptop slightly to the left and produced a notebook. The page it opened on contained illegible scribbles covering every page. Nick uttered a small cough into the back of his hand and then began.

"The Smiling Woman' myth/legend appears to have originated from Japan in the 1300s, what we perceive as 'Medieval Japan'. This version of the tale focuses on a young woman by the name of Koharu. Koharu was one of the most beautiful women in Japan, and many men asked for her hand in marriage. At that time, the father had possession of his daughters, and he would decide who would be the best husband for his offspring. Koharu's father decided that his daughter would marry Eiichi, a wealthy man who was well respected in the area. This marriage was orchestrated to bring two families of great respect together in Japan. As a young, obedient daughter, Koharu married Eiichi without any protest.

The one thing Eiichi wanted more than anything was a child. A boy to pass his wealth to after his death. However, after a year of trying, it was discovered that Koharu could not bare a child. Eiichi became frustrated with this- taking his wife's inability to have a child as a comment on his own masculinity. He therefore turned the blame on his wife; stating that had he wed any other woman in Japan, he would have a child. Not only did he blame Koharu, he became jealous of every man who would pass Koharu a momentary glance in the street. As I previously stated, Koharu was beautiful and jealousy can turn any man into a monster. Koharu was only permitted to leave the house without his company to gather food from the local market, and at gatherings she was never allowed to leave his side.'

'I apologise for rushing through this story, but I hope you can get the gist.' Sarah nodded again, and cued Nick to continue the story.

'Here the tale becomes more complicated, as some believe that Koharu fell for the young blacksmith in their village, and that they 'courted' in secret when Koharu came to the market. Others

65

believe that one-night Eiichi raped Koharu in blind drunkenness, a situation which became more common as the months went by, forgetting the event the morning after. Whichever version you believe, the result was the same. Koharu became pregnant. Now, on most occasions, such news would bring happiness to the father. However, Eiichi's jealous nature rose within him, forcing him to believe with all his mind that the child was not his.

Upon hearing the news he beat Koharu within an inch of her life and dragged her bruised and battered body into the street for all to see. The blacksmith attempted to come to Koharu's aid, attempting to pry the husband's hands from his wife's hair- that he had clenched in his fist. Although the blacksmith believed that he was acting in a heroic manner; by attempting to help the poor, young wife, he in fact sealed her fate. Throwing Koharu to the ground, Eiichi removed his Wakizashi Tanto short samurai sword from it's sheath. With madness in his eyes, he raised it above his head and brought the sharp blade down into Koharu's stomach, killing the child within. He turned to enact the same revenge on the Blacksmith, but the hero had disappeared in the crowd, never to be seen again. I wish I could say this poor woman's misery stopped here, but it did not.'

'By some sad miracle, Koharu lived. But she survived in horrifying circumstances that no person should be made to live in. Eiichi locked her away in his house, refusing to allow her into the sunlight in case she tempted another man. The only way she could witness the world outside was through a thin crack in the wall of her prison. From which, if she positioned her hand-mirror correctly, she could watch the children of the village play on the grass, hear them laughing and enjoying their innocent youth. At first, Koharu cherished these moments. The laughter lifting her momentarily from the misery she had become accustomed to. However, weeks passed. Months passed. And the laughter that had once brought a smile to her face, now brought a feeling of hatred and envy no human should experience. For that laughter should have belonged to her child. The child that was taken from her.'

'One night, Eiichi came back home from work. The outside world knew nothing of the prison he had constructed for his wife- he had assured them that she was ill and had to remain indoors. The witnesses of the stabbing turned a blind eye to the events of that day, not wishing to bring harm on their own family. After ensuring the front door was locked, and the window shutters covered every opening, he unlocked Koharu's door and waited for his wife to come out from her room. She did not. Eiichi called into the room, ordering his wife to come out, but again- no reply. Eiichi undid the leather belt that held his sheath in place, held it between his two hands and brought the two pieces of leather together with a crash that echoed through the room. With this weapon of punishment in his hand, he entered his wife's room.'

'In the centre of the room was a small wooden chair. Upon it, a woman stood, who once an onlooker would have called beautiful. But not now. Her face had transformed into a haggard white, her teeth a mixture of stained yellow and grey, and her greying hair hung without life on her head. Around her neck was a woven rope connected to the wooden beam that ran across the length of the room. In her hand, a shard of mirrored glass stained a crimson ruby, with blood steadily flowing from Koharu's clenched fist.

'Do you think I am beautiful?' Koharu asked her husband, as an estranged smile grew on her face.

'Get down from there.' Eiichi ordered with a hint of fear creeping into his voice. 'Now! Get down from there!'

Koharu tilted her head to one side, her eyes wild with madness and envy. 'Do you think I am beautiful?' However, this time she brought the shard to the corner of her lips. Her smile faded in an instant to a furious grimace. 'You took my child from me! My child! You took everything from me! I will have my revenge, if not in this life but the next!'

With this, Koharu unleashed a demonic scream that filled the air and forced the shard through her left cheek, and then the right- blood gushing down her arm onto the floor. Koharu closed her eyes and stepped forward off the chair. That is the end of Koharu's story. Or so she had hoped.'

Chapter 13

Sarah sat motionless, her eyes remained unmoving and focused on the image of Koharu on the screen of the laptop, but the cogs in her mind were whirring at a million rotations per second. She had so many questions, but none that felt important enough to transfer from her mind to her lips. Instead she sat muted, waiting for someone to break her from the trance she found herself in.

'May I continue?'

Nick had waited patiently for Sarah to arise from her thoughts for too long, and he felt agitated to continue his story.

'Many supernatural experts that have researched this tale believe that, because Koharu's spirit had been engulfed in fury and vengeance at the moment she took her own life, an otherworldly force sensed the pain and saw an opportunity. This otherworldly force offered Koharu a choice. A choice to either continue down the path she had forged for herself, passing away into the nothingness that is death. Or to be given the chance to return, to reclaim what was taken from her. A child. Koharu mistook this offer as one from God, a second chance at the life she could have had. However, rather than return, she was banished to another- an alternate world if you will. Unable to step foot in this world for an extended period of time, she resorted to luring a child back to her new home using a mirror as a gateway. The first child was an orphan, someone Koharu felt she could provide with a better life.

However, the forces had not brought her back using light magic- but dark. Darker than Koharu had first realised and her second chance at being a mother came at a cost. A desire developed within her, a need that compelled her to take more children. Not satisfied with one child, she began to lure more children into her lair, feeding off the fear that every child exerted like a drug. And like a drug, with each innocent she took, her addiction to that fear became greater. With each child kidnapped, the humanity in Koharu diminished-leaving the mythical demonic figure that we now know as 'The Slit-mouthed woman' or 'The Smiling Woman'.

As time passed, and history forgot about the tragedy of Koharu, she developed the guise of 'Bloody Mary'. When these words are uttered into a mirror, the Woman can sense that vulnerable, scared children are caught in her trap- staring into mirrored glass, trembling with fear. The Woman, for the demonic entity has none of the humanity Koharu possessed, listens for children to utter those three, fatal lines. Before the realisation of what they have summoned, the Woman has captured another child for her collection. Since that day, it is believed that over five hundred children have been taken into this other world by the Woman… and there is no evidence that It will stop.'

'Now, I must transfer to a new chapter in the story and address the blue stone that is in your possession. The blue stone is the only recorded way to travel between our world and the other. The last account that featured the stone was in 1932, by an American man named Johnathon Swerter. He wrote a diary entry describing his intention to travel through a 'gateway' into another world using 'the blue stone'.'

'Did it work?'

'We don't know. He disappeared the next day, never to be seen again and leaving no trace… no trace in this world anyway.'

Sarah's leg began to shake with a mixture of nervous and excited energy, 'Is that how we get Lucy back? The stone?'

Nick nodded and sat back in his chair as tears welled in Sarah's eyes. That nod had cracked the water dam within her, and now all of the emotion Sarah had been holding in for so long burst through. She raised her hands to her face and sobbed uncontrollably. Nick remained sat motionless, unsure of whether to offer some form of affection to the crying woman in front of her, or to stay as he was-watching and hoping she would soon stop. He thought of Data in Star Trek striving to become more human. To Nick, this was foolish and the aim should be to behave more like Spock- controlling the emotion within to maintain composure and logical thought. Luckily for him, Sarah regained control and took several deep breaths-feeling embarrassed that she had broken down in front of this stranger. She looked at the picture of Koharu, then at the mirror, then at Nick.

'When?'

'Well, I think I still need to research how to-'

'I want to do it tonight.'

'I'm not sure if it is safe to-'

'Tonight.'

Chapter 14

Sarah stood before the mirror in the kitchen that belonged to the man she had only met a few hours before. Pounding in her ears, her heart sounded like a marching drum counting the seconds till Sarah would have her daughter back in her arms. A bead of sweat trickled down her forehead and stung as it rested in her eye. Nick was stood beside her, his mouth was moving quickly but Sarah couldn't register what he was saying. Her eyes, mind and heart were all focused on the mirror. She felt something cold move into the palm of her left hand. The blue stone. As the stone came into contact with her skin, she felt an electric pulse either moving from the stone into her hand or from her hand into the stone, she couldn't tell. The electricity Sarah had noticed tingled her fingertips and ran from her fingernails around her body, causing her heartbeat to quicken still.

Without comprehending the instructions Nick had been giving, she knew exactly what she must do. The stone had told her. Her heart had told her. Something moved in the corner of the room, just out of Sarah's vision. A large, dark figure, but she remained focused with the gateway before her. Sarah moved towards the mirror, slowly but with determination. She stood so that her nose lay just before the mirrored glass.

'I am coming for you Lucy.' she whispered under her breath. Her hand tightened on the stone in her palm and she felt the locket around her neck press into her skin to give the owner the strength to proceed into the unknown. Her foot moved forward and the mother stepped through the glass without a moment hesitation.

Sarah let out a scream.

The mirror shattered.

The stone dropped to the floor.

Sarah was gone.

Part Two

Chapter 1

'She isn't awake yet.'

'I guess we will just have to postpone her birthday to another year…'

From beneath the pink blanket, Lucy heard her father mutter these words from near her bedroom door. Lucy remained as still as she possibly could, even trying to hold her breath under the covers. The floorboards creaked as both her Mother and Father edged towards their daughter's bed. Sarah looked over to Michael and smiled. Michael raised his hand with five fingers extended. Slowly, mouthing the numbers along with his actions, he counted from five to one. On one, Sarah and Michael pounced on their daughter playing possum- their fingers extended to tickle Lucy awake. Lucy's gorgeous laugh seeped from beneath the blanket like honey dripping from silk.

'Stop! Stop! I give up! I give up!' she laughed, curling herself into a defensive ball.

'Happy birthday Lucy!' both her parents shouted.

'You should be up by now! Your presents won't wait all day.'

The word 'presents' caused a smile to erupt on Lucy's small, excitable face that could have melted their parent's hearts on the spot. She uncurled herself and bolted down the stairs, skidding on the floorboards as she turned the corner.

'Be careful!' Michael shouted as he began to follow her daughter to the living room. He squeezed his wife's hand tight and smiled again at her.

'Are you ready for the mayhem? We better go down quickly before she has opened all of the presents and disappeared under a sea of wrapping paper.' Sarah looked down at her husband's hand, feeling the love flow from his heart to hers through the warmth of his touch. 'Are you okay Sarah?'.

'Yes… yes, I am fine.', Sarah said snapping out of a daydream, 'I will follow you down.'. Michael nodded and walked out of the room to find his daughter. Sarah turned her attention to the bedding on Lucy's bed and began straightening the cover.

Tap.

Sarah froze.

Tap.

Sarah knew, deep down, this was a dream. Maybe that she was dead and reliving her memories. But she also knew that she did not want to look behind her.

Tap.

Slowly, Sarah turned her head. Her eyes had barely registered the figure behind her before a skeletal hand had tightened around her throat. Sarah looked at the figure in front of her. The Smiling Woman from the pictures, a bloodied slit from cheek to cheek. The grip became tighter until Sarah struggled to force breath into her lungs.

'Do you think I am beautiful?'

Sarah tried to speak, tried to answer the demonic being in front of her, but all of the air had been forced out. The Woman's grip tightened further and then her hand twisted Sarah's head like a rag doll.

Crack.

Awaking suddenly, her body was on fire- with every hair standing up on end and her every muscle screaming in pain. Sarah felt the cold tiles of Nick's kitchen floor beneath her hands and her heart dropped to the pit of her stomach.

'*It hasn't worked*', she thought to herself, '*It hasn't bloody worked!*'

Blinking a few times, she waited for her vision to clear. Allowing her vision to gaze around the room for Nick, anger filled her veins as she searched for the 'expert' who would receive the brunt of her disappointment and anger for believing his story. The room was empty. No Nick, no table and chairs, no laptop, only the mirror in the centre of the room.

This must be some sort of practical joke he is playing. Well, it is certainly not funny.

Sarah could feel the anger becoming fury within her.

'Nick! Where are you?', she shouted into the empty room. No answer. Her voice sounded different, almost louder than she expected it to, like the air was reacting differently to her exclamation. 'Nick!' she shouted again, louder this time as her anger grew. Sarah heard movement from the adjoining room.

'Got that fat fucker.' she thought and raised herself to her feet. Having experienced many a hangover before, Sarah expected a headache to seep into her skull after hitting the tiled floor with force, but the rush that met her head as she stood was unlike anything suffered before. She rested herself back down on the tiled floor for a moment, before trying, more successfully this time, to rise to her feet. With each foot feeling like they weighed three times their usual amount, Sarah moved towards the door that led into the other room. Her hand rested on the door-handle, but something compelled her to pause. Her fingertips tightened on the dirty brass handle. Had anybody asked her, she wouldn't have been able to explain why she didn't barge into the room to find Nick. It was a feeling, deep down, that refused to let her open the door.

Moving her body closer to the door, still without turning the handle, she put her ear to the wood. Quiet, no louder than wind passing through an open window, there was the sound of someone breathing. Not heavily, nor lightly, but a rasping steadily on the other side of the door.

As Sarah leant against the wood listening to this, her eyes inadvertently perused the kitchen again. Now that her eyes had fully acclimatised to the darkness of the room, she noticed that the green wallpaper was peeling where the wall met the ceiling, with a dark mould infecting the wall underneath. The kitchen top, that moments before had held a toaster and kettle, now lay bare- with a thick layer of dust covering the surface.

'This isn't right.'

A chill ran from the brass door-handle, through her right hand and into her heart.

'It worked.'

Sarah suddenly found the urge to smile and laugh out loud, and the laughter almost escaped from her mouth but instead it ran with its tail between its legs, to hide in a dark corner within her mind. A creak from the other side of the door. Without thinking, she released the door handle and moved to one side, with her back against the wall. Not a minute after she had done this, the door swung open and covered her from sight.

Sarah closed her eyes and tried to control her breathing- that now sounded heavier and louder in her ears. She didn't know what had been standing behind that door, but she knew it was not Nick. The floor creaked again, followed by a thud as the thing behind the door stepped forward. Then the sound of something dragging across the floor to where the heavy foot had stopped. The thing paused. Another thud. Another drag. Thud. Drag.

Sarah opened her eyes and forced herself to peer through the small crack in the door. Although she couldn't see much; the outline of a large figure was visible standing next to the mirror in the centre of the room. The thing remained where it was, a hand stretched out towards the broken mirror-almost sympathetically. The thing breathed in deeply and then forced the painful breath back out into the room. Sarah leant closer to the crack in the door to gain a better view.

Creeeeak.

The door moved, no more than an inch, but the creak of the hinges made it sound as though it had moved a metre. Sarah took a sharp intake of breath. Her blood ran cold. The thing tilted it's head towards the door. And smiled.

Chapter 2

Fear desperately caught Sarah's breath in her throat. Her body went cold, freezing her to the spot like a statue. The thing's head was now looking directly at the door, which Sarah was hidden behind. The face was something that without witnessing in person is difficult to describe.

It resembled something human-like, however in place of a nose, the thing had two slits in the centre of it's face- like that of a snake. One almost entire white eye looked out from one socket with a narrow slit of black in the middle. The other eye lay not within the socket, but across it's yellowish tinged cheek, attached to the socket by entwined purple veins. Although the eyeball swung uncontrollably from the momentum at which the thing's head had turned; the thin slit of a pupil continued to shrink and enlarge as any pupil would. The mouth possessed no lips, but rather thin green lines around a hole containing numerous dagger-sharp teeth arranged with two large teeth at in the middle. The thing's hair lay in four long singular strands down the face and reached almost to the floor.

Sarah remained, breath caught, staring into the one pearl white eye of the creature through the gap in the door. The creature looked directly back into her own blue eye. They remained in a stale mate, each waiting for the other to make the first move towards their pistol to make the first shot of the duel. A bead of sweat fell from Sarah's face.

Before the bead had hit the floor, the creature pounced. Without thinking, Sarah pushed the door outwards and caused the thing to collide with the solid wood. The creature let out a primal scream, so horrifyingly un-human Sarah raised her hands to her ears to protect them.

The creature snarled, green drool gathering around the corners of it's mouth and sharp teeth. Sarah could now see that the thing didn't possess a human figure at all, but rather from the waist down the body morphed into a serpent's tail with a rattling end, which began to shake uncontrollably with envy.

The thing pounced again. This time, without a door to protect her, Sarah launched herself into the centre of the kitchen and collided with the smashed mirror. The thing's smile widened. It slowly slithered towards Sarah, the rattling tail vibrating furiously as it crept closer. It clicked it's forked tongue and for one final time launched towards Sarah to delve it's fangs deep into her flesh.

Sarah scrambled across the floor, searching with her hands to find something, anything, to protect herself from the beast's dripping fangs. Her hand closed around a shard of broken mirrored glass, and she raised it in defence just in time for the thing to pounce, not realising that a weapon had been drawn. The shard of glass sliced through the serpent's tail with ease and yellow liquid poured out onto the floor. The thing reeled back; shock encapsulated in it's one eye. It looked down at the wound, then at it's prey. Without thinking, instinct taking over, Sarah moved forward and sliced again with the shard of glass. The creature shrieked in pain as it's dangling eyeball dropped to the floor. With one last snarl, the thing projected itself out of the kitchen window and smashed into the dark night outside. Sarah looked at the broken window, then at the glass shard in her hand. The breath that was still hiding in her throat suddenly forced itself into the air, but sounded like a laugh of relief that surprised herself to hear it. The last thing Sarah remembered was seeing the creature's eye rolling on the floor, before her own eyes rolled back in her head and she fell backwards onto the stone tiles unconscious.

Chapter 3

The smell of rotting flesh forced Sarah to regain consciousness and raise her head from the floor. Her clothes were wet through by the creature's yellow blood. She deduced the putrid smell came from this sticky liquid that stained the clothes that hung from her body. The temperature in the room had dropped considerably, due to the smashed window, and she could see her breath fog in the air before her eyes.

'What had just happened?'

Sarah thought about the thing that had attacked her moments before. She had known that whatever lay on the other side of the mirror would not be like her world, but she would never have predicted that she would come face to face with something like that. Sarah wondered if that serpent creature had always been that, or if it had succumbed to the dark forces as Koharu had. Fear whispered into her ear, 'What other horrifying things could be out there?', but Sarah pushed that thought to one side. She couldn't let fear get the better of her- not when her daughter's life was at stake. With a head that felt like it weighed three times the usual, she mustered the energy to stand.

'I need a drink... In fact, I think this is the longest I have been without a drink for a long while.' This thought could be used to explain the pounding feeling within her head. Although, as of yet, the adrenaline coursing through her veins pushed down any withdrawal symptoms.

Instead, the overwhelming feelings that did make itself known was through her stomach- as it rumbled quietly. Not too loud, striving to become the centre of attention, but loud enough that Sarah took notice. There was no clock in this version of Nick's kitchen, but she felt that she had been in this place for more than three hours- and she had not eaten before visiting Nick's house.

Moving to the cupboard in the otherwise bare kitchen she opened the door. Nothing. The only thing that she found within was a blanket of dust with minute footprints moving from one side of the shelf to the other- most likely belonging to a cockroach of some description.

Leaving the door open, Sarah moved her attention to the room adjoining the kitchen, that once housed the serpent creature with the dangling eyeball. The room was dark, but Sarah could make out outlines of furniture that gave her hope. If there were pieces of furniture, the lounge area had been used more than the kitchen, which meant there was a higher likelihood of food or drink.

'I would kill for a gin right now.'

Sarah walked towards the open door, bending momentarily to pick a piece of mirrored glass off the floor as a precaution. There was a light switch on the inside wall of the room, which Sarah clicked on tentatively. As soon as the light flickered into life, Sarah saw the contents of the room and took a step backwards.

Sarah had been right about there being furniture, as in the room a solitary recliner sofa stood in the centre of the room facing an old dusty television set. However, this was where normality finished as in front of the chair lay the remains of a human carcass. The person's ribs lay bare and stained with dry blood, and the head appeared to be torn open from forehead to chin. Sarah brought her empty hand to her mouth and forced the vomit forming back into her stomach. In the corner of the room appeared to be a pile of discarded clothes.

'It obviously didn't like to eat it's meal in the wrapper… Had this person be taken from my world?'

After scanning the room for any other form of food, Sarah moved carefully towards the pile of clothes, remaining constantly aware that something may still be lurking in the shadows of the room. Once there, she bent and began ruffling through the pockets of countless jackets and trousers for anything useful.

'Bingo.'

Sarah's hands touched the edge of a cereal bar plastic wrapper in one of the pockets and brought it out. The bar appeared squashed and the package was slightly torn at the corner but Sarah couldn't complain- especially when she didn't know when or where her next meal would come from. Her luck may not continue and who knew what world may be waiting outside of this house.

Ripping the package open with her teeth, Sarah engulfed the bar eagerly. Her stomach grumbled in appreciation and allowed her to continue rifling through the pockets of prey that had passed through this house previously. In one pocket Sarah found a mobile phone with no battery.

'Who would she call anyway in this world? I am alone.'

In another, she found a keychain which held two keys- these she assumed belonged to a house and car. The final item Sarah's hand found was a small, blue pen knife with a blunt blade.

'It is better than nothing. Now, I need a plan.'

She stopped herself.

'What am I doing? I'm not skilled enough for this… I am an alcoholic ex-teacher. How am I going to be able to find my daughter in a world like this? I don't even know what might be out there. How could I be this stupid? I should have stayed… I shouldn't have listened to that man. My daughter might not even be out there! How do I know? I am following a dream, on a whim that it might be true. And how can I get back home? The stone is gone and that fat man certainly won't put his life at risk for a stranger. My husband… ex-husband… will probably think I have thrown myself into the nearest river… Maybe I should have…'

Sarah clenched her fist and once again, shook the fearful thoughts from her head.

'Lucy might not be out there. But I need to find out. Without her, there is no world worth going back to.'

Once she was sat in the leather chair in the centre of the room, she closed her eyes so that she could work out her next move. She knew Lucy was being held captive in an orphanage, but she didn't know where or, in fact, if she was still there, or if she was ever there. Also, more prominent in her mind, was the thought that there may be more monsters like the creature she had met in this house. She had no idea what may be waiting for her outside of this house. Judging from the pile of clothes in the corner of the room, the poor, unfortunate people who may have ventured into this world had not fared well against the locals.

First step, to find a library. Although this house was not the

81

identical replication of Nick's in her world; the house did remain here. Therefore, Sarah could assume with a small amount of confidence that outside of the door was a clone of her world, a mirror world, where she would be able to find the Stratford-Upon-Avon library. There, she could find the location of the orphanage and, perhaps during her travels, find other resources such as Aspirin for her pounding headache.

After nodding her head as if in agreement with her own plan, Sarah stood and made her way to the front door. With one hand grasping the rusty penknife with the blade erect, and her heart beating with the rhythm of her throbbing headache, she put her other hand on the door handle.

'Three...two...one.'

The door opened. A new world awaited her. With a deep breath and one foot forward, Sarah closed the door behind her and went in search of the only thing that could inspire such confidence within a mother. Her daughter. Her Lucy.

Chapter 4

Detective James Bannister looked down at his black leather-bound notebook. So far, his notes consisted of merely the name 'Sarah Bell' and the word 'Missing'. After the call had been made by her neighbour to the council, that her mailbox was overfilled and complaining that the woman was a 'Disgrace to this neighbourhood', James' boss had asked him to make a curtsy call to the residence-leaving the more serious cases for the detectives that he respected (and those who didn't defy his direct orders to pursue cases that were closed). James had been rather nervous as he walked towards Sarah's apartment door because the last time they had met, it had suggested that her daughter would return within the next few days and James had been ordered to ignore the case.

Over the next few years, James had continued to keep tabs on missing children cases- hoping to be able to bring the grieving parents some news. The mounting missing children cases across the country had begun to suggest that perhaps the separate cases could be linked. James had begun to gather evidence, until one day the Captain had discovered the file. So filled with arrogance and pride in his position, James had been ordered to stop wasting resources making connections where there were none. This came as a direct order, and if James did not obey, his privileges would be revoked, and he would be demoted to community officer.

Many years later, James felt a stone in his stomach thinking about the Bell case as he knew, deep down, that he could have done more to help the family. The thought of what the years may had done to

Sarah didn't bare thinking about.

Regardless, James knocked on the door- to no answer. He had tried the door handle to find that it opened with ease, allowing him to peer into the dirty apartment. Adding weight to the stone in his stomach, James could see the cascaded pill capsules and alcohol bottles on the floor. However, there had been no sign of Sarah.

Knowing that had he asked his superior on the next action to take, James would have been 'advised' to leave the case, presuming that the distraught mother had taken herself to a riverbank and tossed herself in- therefore not to waste his time and department money on such a case. But he didn't ask his superior. Instead, he located the home of her now ex-husband Michael Bell and made his way to find out whether he knew where his divorced wife had disappeared to. Whether James acted in this way due to a strong moral code, or due to the guilt that sat perched on his shoulders every day since the daughter had disappeared, he could not say. What he did know was that now, fate had brought Detective Bannister back into the lives of the Bell family and that he would help in any way he could to ensure they didn't suffer any more grief.

As his small Fiat Panda pulled into the driveway of Michael Bell, James couldn't help but wonder whether, if they had been spared of losing their daughter, their marriage would have continued. Or whether there had been issues lying beneath the surface that arose when it saw the opportunity.

The house before him was larger than he expected, with a modern exterior and a striking red painted picket fence around a front garden. As James walked up the paved pathway to the house, he admired the roses that crept up the edge of the fence- a mix of white, pink and red, that each strived to be in prime viewing of the house's visitors. He peered through the curtained window next to the door to see if anyone was inside. Although he couldn't make out much; James could see a light on in the rear of the house.

James knocked on the door. No answer. With the dreaded feeling of de ja vu, he knocked a second time- hoping that he wouldn't be greeted with the same image inside as he was at Sarah Bell's apartment. James heard shuffling from behind the door.

'I'm coming. I'm coming.', came a voice from within.

James let out an audible sigh of relief. Although he didn't know what he expected Michael's appearance to be like; the well-kept garden and newly painted fence had provided him with some hope that Michael had found a life beyond his daughter's loss. The man that opened the door and greeted him with a smile on his perfectly shaven face still shocked James, as he looked better than he could have imagined under the circumstances. So much so, that if the detective had been working the case of the missing Bell daughter now; the father would have been featured at the top of the list of suspects.

'Good morning officer, what can I do you for?', he asked politely. He then looked at his watch on his wrist and looked back at James. 'I am afraid I must be going out to work soon, I am a teacher at the local school you see. Not that I am trying to rush you or anything, it is just I have to make sure my classroom is ready.'

James snapped out of his daze and regained control of the bewildered look that had crept onto his face.

'Good morning sir, I am sorry to bother you. My name is Detective James Bannister, you may remember me from-'

'You were there in the police station, weren't you?' A mixture of fear and anger had crawled into his voice and it wavered ever so slightly as he reached the end of his question.

'Yes... yes I was. I am ever so sorry.'

'Nothing to be sorry for now. She is gone.' This was spoken abruptly and quickly, reminding James that this man had lost a daughter and no one could ever get over such a thing- no matter how much plaster had been spread of the cracks in his life with his new house, well-kept garden and freshly shaven face. 'What are you here for Detective? That case was closed.'

'Who is there darling?' Walking down the stairs behind Michael was a young, attractive woman dressed in a loose, white blouse with a bag full of school workbooks in her left hand. She noticed James standing in the doorway and walked slightly quicker to the door. James found it interesting how, even though a person may possess a completely innocent conscious, they still behave guiltily around officers of the law. 'Oh, good morning officer. Is everything okay?'

'Yes darling, thank you. Why don't we take separate cars to work today? I won't be long, but if I am slightly late I don't want you to be late as well. We won't be long, will we detective?'

'No... No, shouldn't be long at all.'

The woman looked at Michael, then back at the detective, a million questions on her tongue, but she kept them locked behind her jaw. Instead, she smiled and pecked Michael on the cheek with a gentle kiss.

'I will see you at school.' the woman said and slid her way past James in the doorway. James didn't turn around, but he heard the car door open and close, and then the engine start.

'Would you like to come in detective?'

'Yes, thank you. As I said- I won't take too much of your time.'

James closed the door behind himself and followed Michael through to the living area. The house appeared well kept, with fresh flowers in the vase beside the entrance to the living area. The walls were a rich, cream colour- which contrasted well with the red carpeted floor. It reminded James of the model homes that are made to entice people to buy their properties. Although they look homely; they are not a person's home- merely the outer shell that can be filled with memories of the future. This house had not been filled with any memories. The walls remained pictureless, the carpet remained in pristine condition. James could tell that Michael had actively tried to move on with his life but had found it more difficult than he showed. They both sat on a leather sofa and, after a moment for Michael to settle into the seat, James began.

'I am truly sorry to bother you sir. I am following up on a missing person case, concerning your ex-wife Sarah.' At the mention of 'missing', Michael had become alert- his whole body reacting to the word by turning to stone. 'We received a complaint from her neighbour two days ago, about the fact that her post box was overfilled and that no one had moved in or out of her flat. Normally, we leave such matters for a few more days as they resolve themselves. However, this neighbour was rather…insistent. I visited the premises to find that no one was home. The door was found open and inside it appeared no one had been home for a while. Judging from the letters in her mailbox, I would assume the premises had been vacant for about a week. I was wondering if you had heard from her in that time? Whether she had contacted you at all?'

Michael sat motionless for a few minutes, his mind whirring with concerns and queries. Finally, he said-

'No. No, she hasn't contacted me at all. I mean… the last time I saw her was years-', he stopped himself, 'Actually, she visited… visited about a week ago. Yes. She…she wanted to talk to me about Lucy. Said that she had seen her. Not in person mind, in her dreams. She didn't seem all there if I am honest with you detective. Sarah wanted me to come with her, to visit someone- an expert- to contact

Lucy. Of course, I declined. And since then… nothing. I assumed she went to this man, had her palm read or whatever, and then went back to her usual life.' A look of guilt flitted in Michael's eyes as he realised that he may have been the last person to see Sarah before she disappeared.

'Could we go back slightly Mr Bell? You said that 'she didn't seem all there'. What do you mean?' Michael thought carefully about his response to this, as if he was under questioning in court.

'Well, her hair wasn't brushed…and her clothes were unclean. She was unclean. Smelt of alcohol and her eyes were blood shot. It took me aback to see her like that. I hadn't seen her for years and then…' James wrote the description down in his black jotter, left a line and then asked his final question.

'I only have one more question Mr Bell, then I won't keep you any longer. You said she wanted you to see an 'expert'. Who was he? Can you remember?'

'…I can't. I am sorry. It was over a week ago and- Wait. Hang on.' Michael reached into his suit pocket and withdrew a battered brown wallet. Inside, he found a small card with neat handwriting across the back. 'Sarah gave me this, in case I changed my mind. It is all on there. I hope that has been of some help… Could I ask a favour? When you do find her, could you… could you give me a call? I'd like to know that she is safe.'

'Of course, Mr Bell. Thank you for your time.'

With that James slid the card into his black jotter and closed it. He had found what he had come for. A new lead.

87

Chapter 5

As James gazed down the pathway to the house belonging to Nick, he couldn't help feel an uneasiness in his stomach. He couldn't place the reason for this feeling, but knew something wasn't right with this place. It wasn't the colour of the fence, nor the sound of the doorbell as he pressed down- but something was out of place. No answer. James was starting to think he didn't have much look with house visits. He rapped his knuckles against the red door.

'Hello? Mr Sharp? Are you in?'

'I haven't seen him yet.'

Startled, James spun round on his heels. The unexpected voice belonged to an old man who had-without making any sound- crept up the path towards the house door and now stood a breath behind him.

'Oh, I am sorry sir. I didn't mean to make you jump. It's just I live next door and I saw you from my window. Thought you must be looking for Nick. I usually see him in the morning, when I go to the paper shop but I haven't seen him in... hmmm let me think... A couple of days. I thought maybe he had gone on holiday or something but was beginning to worry, so I am glad that someone has come to see him. Are you a relative?'

'A detective.' The old man's body shifted, and he forced his old back to straighten and hold him upright.

'Oh! Oh my, has he done something? He always looked nice,

smiled and waved to me every morning, but… between us…I suspected there was something fishy about him. There always is in my experience.'

'Your experience?'

'I am in charge of the neighbourhood watch around here. It is a thankless job, but someone has got to do it. I feel like it is my duty. We are the same I guess detective. Is there anything I can help you with detective?'

'No, thank you. If you would like to go back to your property sir, I will contact you if I need anything further.' James knew that he was going to need to find another way into the house and didn't want this old man standing in his way.

'Ah, okay. I will just be over the fence if you need me. Renter. Nigel Renter is my name.'

The old man nodded and shuffled back down the pathway, looking over his shoulder every few steps. James waited till he had moved off the Sharp premise and then bent to look under the door mat for a spare key. No luck. His eyes gazed around for an artificial rock of some sort that may be a key hider. Still nothing.

'Look under the gnome!' Nigel Renter was stood at the fence marking the very edge of his property, peering over to watch the detective in work.

'Thank you. Please sir, go inside.' Nigel nodded and moved away from the fence, but James knew that he would only move to another vantage point. Seeing the gnome on the corner of the step leading to the front door, James lifted it and found a key underneath. Hearing the click as it inserted into the lock, James turned the key and entered the premise of Nick Sharp.

Chapter 6

Morbidly, the door swung open on its hinges and instantly James was greeted by the hideous smell of death. His fist clenched around the black notebook in his right hand, as if that would be able to defend him against any sort of threat that lay waiting for him. The house was dark. Even though the sun was shining bright outside, no light was able to venture into the property. However, it was more than dark- it was as if all life had been sucked out of the house and replaced by death. The walls were a sadder shade of grey, the carpet lay lifeless on the floor leading from the door, down the hall, to another room.

'Hello?' The voice that left James' mouth was barely audible so he cleared his throat and tried again. 'Hello, Mr Sharp?' A cough from the room at the end of the dead, grey carpet replied. James crept towards the noise. The sound of every step seemed to be magnified in the dead air, making him wince as he put each foot down. From somewhere deep inside the house a ticking clock could be heard, as if counting down the seconds until James reached the door. Counting down the seconds of his life, but seeming to count faster with each tick.

The door to the room was open and James could just make out the outline of a kettle and toaster on a side table. James peered around the door, into what he presumed was the kitchen, in search for the creator of the cough. Sat in a chair at one end of a long table, turned to face away from the door, a figure could be seen hunched over. The figure coughed again causing his whole body to rock forwards and then backwards.

'Mr Sharp?'

'What do you want?' the figure growled, without turning around to greet his visitor. James could feel he wasn't welcome in this man's home, so quickly moved onto his line of questioning.

'I am here to ask you about a woman you met about a couple of days ago. A woman by the name of Sarah.'

'Never met her.'

'I have brought a picture if that will help?' James removed a small profile picture of Sarah from the black notebook and edged closer.

'I said I haven't met the woman. Now fuck off.'

'Could you look at the picture please sir?' James took another step closer, feeling the ticking of the clock get faster, counting down quicker.

'Siiir? Ha! I am no siiiir. No one has ever called me siiiir. I said get out!' James remained motionless where he stood. 'I gave you your chance. You should have taken it!'. The figure rose to his feet and turned his attention to the detective standing nervously in the middle of Nick's kitchen. After he had taken two tentative steps forward to show Nick the picture of Sarah; James took one large step back at the sight of the man in front of him.

The man was clearly no man at all, but rather something hiding within the man-exterior of Nick Sharp. The skin had gained a greenish tinge, with bright purple arteries and veins crisscrossing across the bare chest of the overweight man. The skin fit the body like an oversized, un-ironed shirt, with creases and overlapping folds around the midriff area. Down the centre of the body, running all the way to the top of the forehead, was a deep, jagged cut. Stitches of various sizes were sewn across the incision to join the two parts of the body together. However, the construction of the face suggested the parts didn't line up as exactly as a jigsaw. One eye was slightly bulging from the socket with a white haze creeping over the surface. The other eye, approximately ten centimetres lower than it's companion, had a thick, red ooze dripping from the corner and seemed to be pointed directly at the floor. The mouth had been ripped off, leaving strands of loose flesh dangling from where the upper lip had been located. In the hole that remained, James could see a grotesque smile with greying teeth, surrounded by decaying black skin.

'Did you think that it was your friend sat here? Ha!' The monster moved swiftly around the table as he spoke, surprising him considering the size of the figure that stood before him. 'Flea made this outfit myself. Every last bit of it. Do you like it? Flea has been prisoner on the other side for years, unable to step foot in this world. Until, that is, the previous owner of this body opened a gateway… built a bridge between the two worlds. But I knew Flea couldn't live over here without some sort of protection from this disgusting air. Luckily, this man's skin did just the trick! Ha!'. Each time 'Flea' laughed, a cascade of spittle flew from his mouth into the air, releasing a stench much worse than that of the deceased corpse that it was wearing. 'He made a deal with the overseer… I bet he didn't think the cost would result in his life ending so soon! Silly man. Meddling with things he doesn't understand. A bit like you!'

James moved around the table, also in time with Flea, making sure the table stayed between them as a barrier. Flea stopped and bent his back slightly, like a lion preparing to pounce. It sniffed deeply, the nose of the skinsuit flapping as the air was sucked into Flea's nose.

'The problem is, Flea haven't made a suit before. It doesn't fit quite as well as Flea hoped. It isn't air tight. But now… looking at you… I think you would make a be just the right size. Now, come here!'

Flea launched himself at James, throwing the table from between them, sending it crashing against the wall. Shards of wood cascading around the kitchen. James fell back with shock onto the floor, trying to push himself away from the monster before him. Flea relished the sight of the frightened detective on the floor. Bringing a fleshy hand across his face to wipe away the spittle, he licked his lips and descended upon the helpless prey to put an end to his life.

Chapter 7

The outside air tasted bitter on Sarah's tongue, as if even the air particles were infected by the evil that had conquered this mirror world. Above her, the sky was an unusual shade of brown, similar to that of sand. This world felt different to Sarah's- this world felt sick. Clutching the car keys in her hand, Sarah walked down the garden path towards the pavement. She moved slowly, looking from left to right to scan the street for anyone like the person/thing she had met in the house. The street appeared deserted and was unnaturally silent- as if sound had fled this place in fear. Even the gravel underfoot crunched in a whisper, scared of what the sound may lure. Halfway down the garden path, Sarah pressed her thumb into the key fob- praying that the car would respond quietly. A car further down the street beeped twice, flashing the back lights, and then fell silent again.

After looking in both directions down the street again, searching for life, she saw nothing. Feeling more confident, and moving quickly, she reached the parked car and opened the door. Sarah wondered when the car door was last opened, when the car had last been driven. The battery must still work for the lights to flash, maybe there was hope for the engine also. Driving would be faster, and potentially safer, to find her daughter. She sat in the car and shut the door behind her. Instinctually, her hand moved the key into the ignition and turned. Sarah regretted it instantly as the car unleashed a horrific scream as the engine tried to arise from the dead. The body of the car shuddered with the effort, but finally came to rest. Sarah clenched her fists around the wheel and was about to scream herself when her eyes drifted to the rear-view mirror. Something had moved. Something was out there. A black figure had appeared at the end of the road, walking slowly but steadily towards the car.

Her hand move to the lock on the car door, and thankfully she heard the locking system click into life. Suddenly, every hair on Sarah's body rose, every blood cell coursing through her chilled and her breath caught in her throat. The black figure was not alone.

Four more came into view in the mirror, each walking with purpose towards the car. As they came closer, their appearance became clearer in the reflection, feeding Sarah's fear further. Each wore a long, black overcoat that swished at their ankles, finishing an inch above polished, black boots. On their face, they each wore a mask that Sarah remembered seeing in history books when studying the Black Death in Highschool. In History class, she had learnt that the doctors had worn masks that resembled a raven- the beak filled with herbs and medical remedies to prevent the doctors being infected by the plague. Each of these figures wore a mask similar to this, with a black hood pulled over the top to conceal the eyes peering out from beneath. In their hands, a staff with a candled beacon on the summit of each. The air. Sarah had tasted it when she first opened the door.

The dead air must be poison or something.'

Sarah looked around the interior of the car, searching for something to protect herself with, and something to cover her mouth and nose with, but it was empty. Peering into the rear of the car, the only thing she could see was a grey coat that the deceased man must have owned. Without any better alternative, Sarah moved herself into the rear of the car, took one last look into the mirror at the advancing Ravens, and buried herself under the long overcoat. She dug in her pocket for the small, blunt pocketknife and clasped it in both shaking hands under the coat- awaiting her fate.

The waiting, unknowing of where the Ravens were, felt like torture. They could be peering into the car right at that moment, ready to strike, and Sarah would be none the wiser from beneath the coat. Trapped. Helpless. A sound came from outside of the car. A clinking of metal- like a key being tapped against the bodywork. Then, another sound. The car handle being pulled. Sarah prayed the lock had worked, that the battery hadn't died with the engine. She heard the handle being pulled again. Nothing. Sarah released a sigh of relief from within her hideaway and listened intently for any communication between the Ravens, but could hear nothing.

Time passed. Sarah couldn't be sure if it had been minutes or hours, but to her they felt like days. Finally, Sarah peered from under the coat. They were gone. Although relief flooded through Sarah, one thing was made extremely clear; this world was dangerous and deadly, and she was not welcome.

Chapter 8

Lying still for a moment longer, she tried to catch her breath, but still felt breathless. She noticed that the car had a glove compartment-

'I should have checked that first.'

- and reached over to click it open. Inside she found a map and an energy bar. Once the one was eaten, she opened the other.

'It really is my lucky day.'

She found not only that the map was of the local area, it was folded onto the exact page of her location.

'This means I won't need to go to the library... If I can just find the best way to the orphanage.'

Ignoring the coincidence of finding both food and a map opened to the exact location, Sarah searched the area for the building she had witnessed in her dream. An orphanage, though she couldn't remember the name. Sarah's heart dropped into her stomach, as she searched desperately for an orphanage on the map, thinking that her only lead had been only a figment of her imagination. Finally, her finger fell on the orphanage. Sarah looked from one finger, marking her location, to the other finger, marking the orphanage. Between them lay the expanse of Stratford-Upon-Avon. By car, the journey would have taken approximately fifteen minutes, but walking would at least double that time.

There were two clear routes to her destination. One would follow the main road around the city, but would take longer and Sarah suspected would be patrolled by more of the Raven things that she had narrowly escaped. The other path would take less time, but would involve walking through the central park, past St Gerald's church and following the river directly to the orphanage. Although Sarah had no idea what would await her on this journey; she knew that time was not on her side and that she needed to reach her daughter as soon as possible. So, in her heart, she knew there was only one option now that she didn't have a car to drive. She reached into the back of the car, and pulled the grey overcoat out. Taking the pen knife, she cut a strip of fabric from the bottom and wrapped it around her mouth and nose. After this, she put the remains of the coat on for warmth, and began her journey into the unknown.

Sarah closed the car door behind her, hearing what she suspected was the door creaking on it's hinges as it shut. However, this sound was not a creak but rather a laugh. A laugh that came from the mirror in the car. A laugh that belonged to her daughter's kidnapper- 'The Smiling Woman'. As, little did Sarah know, she was following the exact path laid out for her, like Hansel and Gretel following the breadcrumbs, right into a trap.

Chapter 9

The grotesque, self-constructed body of Flea lay still on top of his prey. A grunt came from beneath the body. Then, slowly, the body moved to the left- inching it's way until it flipped onto it's back and hit the floor, revealing James underneath with his eyes still firmly shut tight. Hesitantly, he opened one eye to see if his attacker was dead. The other eye joined, and he quickly stood to ensure he put some space between himself and the thing known as 'Flea'. From this distance, James could observe his handiwork- his fountain pen that protruded from Flea's chest. If Flea had not dived upon James with all of his weight; he had no doubt that the pen would not have resulted in the death. Thankfully, the full weight of the monster had balanced on the thin, sharp nib of the pen, forcing it through both the flesh suit and Flea's skin.

Edging closer, he tapped the body with his foot. The body remained still. James edged further back, until he came into contact with the table and sat upon the top- his eyes never moving from the kill. His kill. James fought the impulse of sickness and pushed it back down into his stomach.

'Had this disgusting thing murdered Sarah?'

James had to assume this deduction was correct, but he refused to believe it. There wasn't a body, which meant Flea had not skinned her.

'Perhaps he had eaten her?'

He reached into his pocket to retrieve his phone to call his superiors but discovered his pocket empty.

'Must still be in the car.'

He looked around the dimly lit kitchen for any evidence that Sarah had been in the room. Tucked under the table, balanced the seat of a chair, was a brown, leather handbag. James lifted it from the seat and looked inside, knowing already who the bag belonged to. The driver's license inside read 'Sarah Bell', with a picture in the top left corner. Along with this the bag held; a packet of painkillers, a mobile phone, a pair of keys and a half-used roll of lipstick.

'She must have driven here. How come I didn't see her car parked outside? Perhaps it has been reported by the noisy neighbour and towed.'

He put his hands on the table he was sat on to push himself off and felt the cold metal of a laptop to his right. Still dazed, he pulled the screen up. A PowerPoint programme appeared on the screen titled as 'The Smiling Woman'. With the light from the screen lighting the room slightly, James could see that around the laptop lay pieces of scribbled paper. One in particular drew James' attention more than the others… a piece of paper with one phrase scrawled in the centre. 'The mirror is the key'. James reached out, pushed the small, blue stone paperweight off the paper and brought it closer to the light of the screen. Underneath the title was a message written so small that James had to squint to read it. At first glance, the message may have been missed entirely, but once read it sent shivers down his spine. 'The woman is always watching'. Instinctively, James looked over his shoulder but found no-one there. The only company James had in the room was the body of Flea on the kitchen floor.

Not wanting to spend any excess amount of time in the house, James collected the pieces of paper off the table, stacked them neatly with the laptop, and then picked all of the evidence up to put in his car. Just as he reached the door of the kitchen to leave, he stopped. A feeling had come over him, the same feeling he experienced when he had forgotten his car keys. He looked back at the room and noticed the paperweight watching him from the tabletop. Although James could not put his finger on the reason; the paperweight looked out of place in the kitchen. But more than that, it looked out of place in this world. He quickly walked back to the table- put the small, blue stone into his pocket- and left Nick's house without looking back at the thing lying unmoving in the middle of the kitchen. James had every intention to notify his superiors of the attack that had occurred, but he never got the chance.

Chapter 10

The journey from the car to the park took Sarah less time than she had thought. As Sarah had previously predicted, the world she found herself in was near-identical to the one she came from. Near-identical, as any mirror-world would be. Although the houses were in the same place and the trees still lined the edge of the pavement; they were different. Whether it that the brown stonework on the houses at home was now a dark grey, or whether it was the trees that appeared somewhat lifeless- with bare branches reaching towards the sky, asking for help (or to put it out of its misery). As she walked, the intruder of this world tried to keep her head down and focus on reaching the park. Finding no others walking on the street, her mind began to believe that this town, perhaps this world, had been evacuated, and that it remained as an empty shell of what it had been many years ago. Perhaps, whatever poison is in the air had forced the residents to vacate to a safer area- perhaps that same poison is now working its way into Sarah's lungs. However, the feeling of spiteful eyes watching her from behind dirty windows of the houses never left her. Had Sarah gathered the confidence, she would have glanced at the window of the house to her right, but the feeling of what she may find kept her eyes fixed on the road ahead.

Before too long, the large, black iron gate that once protected the park's luscious greenery from the outside world at night was in front of her. But in this world, the night had taken over, and four of the iron bars had been torn away, leaving an opening in the shield for the darkness to invade the innocent park cowering behind the wall.

The gate rested between two brick pillars that appeared weathered from a great storm, the brown brick crumbling at the base but still trying desperately to remain strong to hold the pillars up. At the base of the left pillar was a symbol drawn in a red paint- a large, red circle with the letter 'C' in the middle. Sarah thought of the graffiti that marked her own apartment block at home in Dudley and thought nothing of it.

'This world must have bored youths as well... or did have.'

Light was beginning to fade, as she watched the grey sky turning darker by the second. She checked over her shoulder that she was still alone, ducked under the gate and entered the unknown before her. Behind her, a smiling face emerged from the darkness and followed.

As Sarah moved swiftly down the gravel path to the other side of the park, the sound of her footfall pushing the small rocks to one side was the only accompaniment to her journey, along with the whisperings of the wind. Or at least that was what Sarah forced herself to believe. Deep down, she knew that the air was still and there was no wind to rustle the bare tree branches around her. Rather, the whisperings belong to something within those branches and overlapped each other so that Sarah could only make out some:

'Someone is here.'

'Intruder.'

'A woman is coming.'

'The mother is coming.'

'Death will follow.'

'A smile will be on her face.'

Mustering courage, Sarah stole a glance but could only see the entwined bare bones of the branches. Sarah continued along the path until she heard:

'The mother has come for her daughter.'

This forced her to steal another glance into the darkness- this time focusing her eyes to see through the blanket which had fallen on the trees. Eight shiny eyes gazed back at her. What she had mistaken for branches were in fact long, thin legs. Eight of these legs were attached to the smooth, rounded body of a spider. Not the regular house spider that Sarah would find in her kitchen, scoop into her hands and release outside. This spider was larger, perhaps larger than a car, with each leg the same size as a fully grown adult.

'This is it.', Sarah thought to herself, 'This is the end.'

'Don't be silly woman, we have no desire to harm you. There are far too many things in this world that will do that.' The spider whispered, as if reading Sarah's thoughts.

'You said...' What Sarah wished to ask was *'How can you talk? Why are you so big? What do you mean by 'far too many things'- how many deadly things live in this world?'* but the most important question rose to the surface, 'How did you know I had come for my daughter?'

'We see many things. Hear many things. This world is poisoned. A poison which changed us... created what we are... ' Although Sarah's eyes never left the spider's eight; she could sense other eyes on her.

'How many are there?'

'We are many... but you need not concern yourself with us. You must hurry. The Smiling Woman is becoming impatient. You don't have much time. She is closer than you might think. To retrieve her, you will have to sacrifice greatly and we will observe with great interest. The choices that are made may change this world... Or may not. Many have came before, but only few have stayed. The question is...what will you do for your daughter?'

'Anything.'

'Then go, Sarah Bell. Quickly. Take the river past the barricade. Do not go through the gate. Go.'

The whisperings stopped abruptly, and the eight eyes of the spider retreated back into the shadows without another sound. Sarah turned back to the path in front of her, a renewed determination fixed in her heart. The spider had said that time was running out, so there was no time to waste.

'And they said there are other things in this world, worse than what I have seen already.'

Quickening her pace, Sarah continued along the gravel path through the trees, listening to the sound of her footsteps once more. The eerie silence of the park held a sadness, with the echo of what had once been shouting from the silence- the memory of laughing children refusing to be forgotten.

'Perhaps I am going crazy. The poisoned air might be infecting my mind. I can't spend too long here... But how will I return to my world?'

Trying to shake the thoughts from her mind, she continued on her journey- until Sarah noticed something unusual about the sound of her footfall. It was almost as if each step had an independent echo, another step joining it. There was an shadow to her footsteps.

Something was following in hers, walking with the exact same beat- or trying to. Sarah's pace quickened slightly, but so did her stalker's, always stepping when she did. Without stopping, Sarah looked over her right shoulder, but her vision in the darkened light could only make out twenty steps behind her, where she could see no-one.

Her concentration on her stalker had distracted her from what lay ahead, and as she turned her attention back the path, she saw what seemed to be a light behind the trees. The light moved across the sky and reminded Sarah of the searchlights used in World War Two- scanning the sky for enemies. Although the trees hid where the light was coming from; Sarah knew in her stomach that it wouldn't be good.

'I should have followed the main road. Why did I think it was a good idea to come this way?'

Stopping dead in her tracks, she turned to face the way she came, waiting for her stalker to reveal itself. But the stalker's footfalls stopped abruptly also. Sarah now stood staring into the shadows that had now crept forwards to ten steps away. Whatever was hiding behind that barrier was watching her. Waiting.

'Hey! Whatever is following me, stop it now. Just turn around and go.' This order was meant to sound commanding but as it left Sarah's lips, it sounded more like a whimper. 'I know you are there!'

'Maybe the spiders have decided against letting me go on. Maybe they have got hungry... All of those eyes watching me...'

There was a shift of gravel from the darkness, confirming her suspicions- although this knowledge brought her no comfort. Suspecting a horrible thing under your bed as a kid is not as scary as if you see a hand emerging to drag you beneath. Then, came a noise that Sarah didn't expect.

Honk.

'What was that? A car horn? No... Not quite...A air horn? It must not be the spiders after all. But what had they said? There are things worse in this world.'

Sarah's brow creased as confusion buried itself into her forehead.

'Hello?' Sarah replied- peering with all her might into shadows before her. Another honk came from the shadows, followed by a high-pitched laugh- devoid of everything joyful that makes a laugh such a wonderful sound.

'Do you think this is funny?' Sarah asked, gaining confidence from the cowardness shown by her pursuer still hiding behind the dark, 'Do you think scaring a woman in the dark is something funny?'

A face emerged into the light. The thing hiding in the house had frightened her, the giant spiders had scared her, but the face that appeared chilled Sarah to the bone. A pale white face of a clown, with blue circles painted around it's eyes and a large red mouth drawn in a smile from cheek to cheek. It wore a large red clown nose and lime green hair hung down the sides of it's head. Following the head, it's body stepped forward- revealing a dirty, stained white clown outfit, with pink pom poms down the centre, and large, scuffed purple shoes. From first appearance it looked human, but Sarah felt deep down that the humanity had long since left this person. Whatever poison that resided in the mirror world had corrupted any humanity, leaving the entity before her. The clown's smile grew, pushing it's painted smile further across it's cheeks.

'Boo!'

Chapter 11

The clown lurched forward, with its white gloved hands outstretched to grab Sarah, but she had already turned and was running down the gravel path towards the bright searchlight. Hot on her heels, the clown was running close behind with saliva dripping from its mouth. Although the clown wore large, oversized purple boots; it moved with tremendous speed and grace.

Quickly, Sarah turned to see how close the clown was to catching her. As she turned her head, her foot caught a rock and sent her sprawling to the floor. The gravel tore into her hands and the pain danced on her palms like needles pricking at her skin. Sarah swore under her breath and pushed herself onwards towards the light. The clown was closer now, and she could feel that it's hunger had grown from the smell of the blood on her hands by the low growling that came from her pursuer. Her attention was focused on the opening of the trees, but she could sense eyes watching her- concealed by the trees. Some of these may have been more of the spiders in the trees, but somehow she knew that other creatures had joined to watch the chase. Sarah's heart was beating fast, the sound thudding in her ears, her legs screaming in agony but understanding that they must push on. Her options were either fight or flight, and she knew the previous win against the creature in Nick's mirror-house had been based purely on luck. This time, she may not be as lucky.

The opening of the trees came closer and closer, her hope

increasing with each step, when suddenly she broke out of the trees and realised she had acted in exactly the way the clown had wanted. Her pursuer had pushed her down the single string of silk into the middle of the spider's web- ready to be wrapped up, injected with venom, and devoured.

In front of her, a large circus tent with blue and red stripes stood resolutely in the centre of a field. The search lights she had seen before was still moving backwards and forwards before the tent, but rather than searching the skies, the main purpose was to attract guests to it's show- 'The Greatest Show in the World' according to the banner that was strung above the opening of the tent- the last show that any of the guests would attend. Sarah took all of this information in as she continued to run down the gravel path towards the entrance. Knowing she had nowhere else to go, no other path to follow, she had to keep moving. To stop would be suicide.

'Get her!' a voice shouted from behind. The sound of eight or nine feet had joined the chase and their pace had increased. As sweat poured down her face and the blood dripped from her palms, she felt as a fox would when being hunted by dogs. A fox can outrun one dog, but now countless more had joined the pack and the fox's chances of survival had dropped from low to near nil. Still, the fox continued to run, keeping the hunt alive and the dogs hungry.

Her eyes scanned the open field for the exit to the park, and with dread, realised her exit lay behind the large tent. She wouldn't survive if she ran for the gate, she needed to lose her chasers first.

'Fight or flight.'
The way back to the woods would be impossible. If she could weave her way through the oncoming Clowns, who knows what may lurk there. And there were too many to make a stand on the open field- Sarah wouldn't stand a chance. There was only one solution. Sarah ran straight into the circus tent, willingly going to the centre of the web- in the hope she could outsmart the salivating spiders on her heels.

The inside of the tent was empty- all the clowns must be searching for their dinner in the park. Audience chairs circled a splintered, wooden podium in the centre of the stage area. Piles of boxes lay on the far side of the stage to the entrance (presumably once containing the stage equipment and props), and a lonely trapeze swung aimlessly above. She ran across the stage, her feet crunching on the surface of the floor- but Sarah didn't dare look down at what made this noise. At the nearest box, she flung the lid up and looked inside. The box contained a brownish straw, but was otherwise empty. However, before seeking refuge within, Sarah thought better of it and moved to a box further back.

'If they start searching the boxes, I don't want them to find me in the first one… It may buy me a little time. Not a lot, but a little.'

She climbed in and closed the lid just as the army of clowns entered the tent, saliva and drool dripped down their chins. They were hungry.

Chapter 12

'Where did she go?'

'How should I know! You saw exactly the same as me. She is in here somewhere. She must be.'

'Can you smell anything?'

'No. Can you?'

'Only faintly. The bitch must have gone. We would be able to smell the blood if she was still here.'

'There is… something… I can smell it faintly. If she has gone, we must have just missed her.'

'Wait… Those boxes. They've moved.'

'How do you know?'

'That lid was open before. It is closed now…'

'I think you're being a bit paranoid- '

'Shut up and trust me. She's here.'

'Do you think she is in one of those?'

'Where else is she going to be!'

Crunch. Crunch. Crunch.

Bang.

'No. It's empty.'

Bang.

'Are you going to go through every single one? She's gone. Just except it. Another meal lost.'

Bang.

BANG!

'Told you so.'

'Fine. Go and see if she has snuck into the forest or if anyone else has seen her. If they have her, she's mine. Understand?'

'Yes… Yes, of course.'

Crunch. Crunch. Crunch.

Sarah let out a sigh of relief as quietly as humanly possible. She opened the lid tentatively and peered out of the small crack. The clowns must have gone. Sarah began to raise the lid more to get a better view, when suddenly the lid was forced back down. A lock fasten over the front of the box.

'I knew you were in one of these, you stupid girl. And now, you are all mine! Do you realise what you are hiding in?'

Sarah looked around herself at the box she was trapped in. A slit followed the centre of the box around each side.

'Oh, it has been a while since I have used this… It is a magician's box. I used to have an act using this that made the audience audibly gasp! I would lock my assistant in and reveal a long saw to the audience. Then, I would put this to one side and withdraw my true weapon for the act. Not many people had seen a woman sawn in half with a chainsaw. Ha!' Sarah heard the clown retrieve an object from the floor. Without seeing, she knew what weapon the clown held in his white gloved hands. 'It is a bit rusty now… still has a shine to it though. I used to love of the stage lights reflected on the audience as I raised it above my head. I can't think of anything more suitable for the occasion. Can you?'

The clown laughed.

A chainsaw sounded.

'I am so very hungry.'

Sarah heard the chainsaw being lifted above the clown's head. The whir of the motor was defeaning. She closed her eyes, tears dripping down her cheek.

'I am sorry Lucy… I am so sorry.' the mother whispered. With fists clenched, she waited for the inevitable. But-

Crack.

Silence.

The sound of the chainsaw stopped suddenly, and she heard it clatter to the ground. After a moment listening for the clown, she tried the lid of the box. It opened with ease. Peering over the side, she saw the lock on the floor surrounded by a sickly green and red liquid. Next to lock, the clown's body- with its painted eyes staring directly at her. Sarah sprawled out of the box and scrambled to her feet, ready to fight for her life. But the clown lay unmoving still. Then, Sarah noticed that, although the face of the clown was facing her; the body was not. The clown's neck was broken and twisted, leaving the clown with a grotesque dead smile across it's lips.

'Had another clown killed it?'
Sarah looked around her quickly for the assailant who had saved her life, but the tent remained empty. Whatever had killed the monster before her had disappeared as quietly as it had arrived.
'Like in Star Wars… there is always a bigger fish.'
Leaving the body lying there, with more questions than answers on her mind, she slid under the outer cover of the circus tent. Through the darkness, Sarah sprinted to the gate leaving the park. Same as the other gate, it had been broken and Sarah could easily fit through the bars. On the wall to the left of the gate, Sarah could make out the 'C' sign again. Now she knew it was not graffiti but a warning. This was Clown property. However, the clown's numbers were down by one. And although Sarah didn't know who or what had saved her life; she knew that had it not, she would not currently be in one piece. She owed this mystery saviour a massive debt. And her saviour would collect it.

Chapter 13

As James drove back to his house, his mind was a blur. The sky was dark and rain poured down, cascading off the front window. Sweat dripped from his brow and into his eyes causing him to squint at the road ahead between the wipe of the window wipers.

'What have I just seen? What have I just done? Have I murdered a man?'

James shook that thought from his head immediately. He had killed something, but it was not a man. Not only that, whatever it was had attacked him first, it was in self-defence.

'But would a court believe that? He had been the one to enter the property, without permission or a warrant.'

Bzzzzzzzz.

With one hand on the wheel, James reached to his trouser pocket to retrieve his phone that was vibrating against his thigh. It slid out into his palm and his eyes drifted from the road to the phone screen. A message from an unknown number came up beside the message icon.

'I need to see you. Come to my house at about 7am. Michael Bell.'

James re-read the message over. 'I need to see you'.

'What has Sarah's ex-husband discovered? Has he come into contact with a similar monster that had taken Nick's skin as a suit?'

These questions span around the carousel of James' mind, taking him into a daydream as he tried to organise his thoughts.

'Whatever was in that room wasn't human. What had the scrawled message said… about the Smiling Woman. Maybe that is the person I need to find.

Perhaps she is the one who kidnapped the Bell's daughter. This isn't a normal case. I know it isn't. There is something going on, and Sarah had worked that out. Whatever information she had gone to Nick's for, it had been found. Had it killed her? No... no, I don't think so. I think only Nick had fell victim to that... thing.'

James' eyes drifted to the stone that sat in the passenger seat on top of the other items he had taken from Nick's house. Without eyes, the stone seemed to return his gaze, tempting him with it's attractive blue colour.

'I don't think that is an ordinary paperweight.' James muttered to himself. If James had remained focused on driving his car, he may have gazed into the rear-view mirror to see if any car were following him. He may have seen not a car, but a woman sat in the rear seat, her eye's piercing white through the dark and a sliced smile across her face. James may have also realised that his wheel had turned slightly to the right, drifting into the opposite lane. Straight into the path of an oncoming car. But James didn't realise any of this before it was too late.

Chapter 14

Beep. Beep. Beep.

James struggled to open his eyes to the burning fluorescent light. Above him was a white panelled ceiling with a long beam light down the centre. Once the pain of the light had subsided in his eyes, he felt the aching that crawled over his body. James winced and closed his eyes again, drifting back into a medication fuelled sleep.

Beep. Beep. Beep.

This time, when James opened his eyes, it was easier. He felt more strength flowing through his body and lifted his head slightly. From this new position, he could see his body lying underneath a thin green sheet on a hospital bed. The room was small- a small side table and an empty chair sat on his left and a range of medical equipment sat on his right. There was no window, nor television in the room- but at the base of the bed, positioned centrally on the wall was a wide framed mirror. James peered into it's depths and breathed a sigh of relief. Whatever the reason he lay in this bed, his face was left relatively unharmed. The memory of what had happened before he had opened his eyes in the hospital room was a blur. He remembered leaving Nick's house, driving back when something had caused him to look away from the window.

'A crash. I must have been in a crash.'

However, something was different about the image that was looking back at him from the mirror at the base of his bed. James had always been nervous about mirrors. As a child, he could remember spending time staring at his reflection, moving his arms trying to catch his reflection out- thinking that if he moved as quickly as he could, the mirror image wouldn't be able to keep up. Although he knew it impossible; he could have sworn that every now and again the reflection would be just a millisecond behind- before it regained pure mimicry.

Now, gazing at his adult self-lying in a hospital bed, he felt uneasy. Like he was peering into a room he shouldn't. The reflection's head twitched.

'Had my head moved?'

James looked over to his right at the medical equipment- it must be the drugs that were currently being pumped throughout body. The heart monitor's blank screen observed the patient on the hospital bed.

'It is turned off… Why is it turned off?'

A thin layer of dust lay over the black screen, as if it hadn't breathed life for years. James looked back at the reflection and felt a cold chill run up his spine. James' face had remained unchanged. The reflection smiled.

The reflection's teeth were a mixture of yellow and brown and his lips were cracking as the smile spread further. Blood began to seep from the cracks and trickle down his chin.

'It must be the drugs.'

But James didn't believe that. He tried to move his body upwards to get off the bed, to get away from the mirror and find help but felt resistance. Around his wrists and ankles were padded restraints tied to the edge of the bed.

'Were they there before?'

James tugged at the restraints again, his eyes never leaving the reflection, but the restraints held strong and bound him to the bed frame. The reflection copied James' movements- but whereas he had met resistance, the reflection sat up in his bed with no restraints to hold him. James' heart drummed faster. The reflection's head cocked to one side again.

'Could he hear my heart beating faster?'

The reflection slid a long, black tongue over his cracked lips- tasting the blood that had seeped through. Raising a hand before his face, the reflection rotated his fingers, with each knuckle cracking one by one. This hand moved to the side table and picked up a small metal object. Although James couldn't see it clearly; he knew it was a scalpel from the sharp edge glinting under the light. The reflection brought the scalpel to his neck and stopped. James felt the cold metal against his own neck, looking down to see that in his own left hand was now free from the restraint and held a scalpel with it's sharp blade pressing into his skin.

'No… No… Please no.' James muttered to the empty room with nothing but the dead heart monitor to listen to the desperate pleas. The reflection narrowed his eyes, as if disappointed by James' pathetic begs of mercy. The smile on his face transformed into a sneer.

'Leave… this… case…alone…' The reflection forced the words from his mouth as if each was a blade of glass scraping up it's throat.

'What are you? Where is Sarah?'

Unsatisfied with these questions, the reflection shook his head slowly. The black tongue emerged again and tasted the droplets of blood on his lips.

'I warned you.'

The blade pushed deeper and slid effortlessly across James' throat. Blood gushed from the cut, pouring over the green bed cover. James' head remained frozen with shock, the pain not registering in his head until it would be too late. His head dropped forward. Just before he forced his last breath, he heard the reflection laugh.

Beep. Beep. Beep.

James sat up suddenly, eyes wide and breathing heavily. His hands reached to his neck. They came up, un-restrained- to find that there was no cut, no blood, no sign of the reflection's deadly work. He looked straight ahead into the mirror on the wall at the base of the bed, but found a very different sight greeted him. The reflection that looked back had a bruise forming down the right side of his face. There was a stitched cut across his eyebrow and what looked like the beginning of a black eye forming on his left.

'You were lucky.'

James started, and turned his neck quickly to his left- instantly regretting the suddenness of movement as pain ignited and spread up in his neck and shoulder. Michael Bell sat in the chair beside the bed with a machine coffee cup held between his hands in his lap.

'What happened?' James' voice sounds croaky and dry.

I'm not surprised. I just had my throat slit by a reflection.'

'Well, it appears Detective Bannister, that you were texting whilst driving. In the dark and the rain, to make matters worse. Your car drifted into oncoming traffic and…', Michael pointed at the bruised and battered body in the hospital bed.

'It was your text I was reading…' James grunted as a beetroot shade of embarrassment spread over his cheeks. 'So, what did you want to see me about?'

'Are you sure you don't want to rest?'

'How long have I been in here?'

'You have been in about a day. The doctors didn't think you would come around just yet. The officers on the scene saw that my number was the last you contacted, so called me as soon as you had moved into hospital. I didn't know if you had a girlfriend, or someone to contact… figured I'd wait around until you woke up.'

'I have had plenty of rest… What did you want to tell me?' As James asked this, he moved his body up in bed so that he could look at Michael without turning his neck. The reflection copied this movement. 'Before you start, could you do me a favour? That mirror, could you take it down off the wall please?'

'The mirror?'

'Yes please.'

With no other comment or explanation, Michael lifted his body out of the chair and removed the mirror from the wall. He looked at it, and then at James- who had a hint of fear in his eyes as Michael held it in his hands. Michael turned the reflective surface away from them and rested it against the wall, before coming back to his seat.

'Thank you.'

Michael nodded, looking carefully at James- judging whether he might be concussed from the collision, or whether whatever pain killers he had been administered would render this next conversation useless as he was as high as a kite.

'I am fine Mr Bell. Please… what were you going to tell me?'

Michael took a deep breath, trying to decide the best way to divulge what he had seen- without seeming like a madman.

'I have… I don't know… I don't how to say it without sounding like a crazy!'

'Believe me Mr Bell,' James muttered without a hint of humour in his croaky voice, 'The things that I have seen in the past few days… you are talking to the one person who may be more mad than you. We are all mad here Mr Bell.'

'Michael, please call me Michael…', Michael took a deep breath, 'Okay… I will just say it. I got… I got a message. A message from

Lucy.'

'Lucy?'

'My Lucy. My daughter Lucy.'

James' brow creased as he processed the information. Michael saw this reaction and began to rise from his seat.

'I'm sorry. This was a mistake-'

'No. Please, go on.'

Michael didn't return to his seat however. Instead, he began pacing around the small hospital room, like a man teetering on the border of insanity.

'I was brushing my teeth of all things.'

'When was this?'

'The morning before I sent you the message… I bent my head down to rinse my mouth with the water. I came back up and looked in the mirror. The mirror had been clear before you see. When I came up, the mirror… It had… You know when you come out of a shower and the steam covers it? Like that, but there was writing. And not adult writing either, the writing of a child. It said *'Daddy, Mum has come to find me. She needs help. Go to the orphanage'*. You probably think I am making it up but-'

'I don't. I don't at all… The last day has been, well saying it has been eventful would be an understatement. After I left you, I traced Sarah's footsteps- to see if I could find any leads as to her whereabouts. I arrived at the residence of Nick Sharp, the man who Sarah had contacted. The person who had the details to on that card. Only to find something that shook my whole outlook on life, my whole belief system. There was something, a sort of being, in his skin. As in, the thing… a monster… was wearing this man's skin like a coat. Crazy I know. I wouldn't believe it if I had not seen it myself. But there it was, sat in Nick's kitchen. It attacked me but I managed to… I managed to get away.'

'Did it… did it hurt Sarah?'

'That was my original thought. However, in the house I found some papers… research. And knowing that you have had a similar encounter as me with-', James pointed at the mirror facing the wall, 'I think that… pass me my bag will you. Is it in here?'

'Yes, they brought it out of the car and put it by the side of your bed when they brought you in. In case there was anything sensitive in there- casework or anything.'

Picking up the bag up from beside the side table, Michael gave it to James. Wincing, the detective lifted his body up to a more comfortable, seated position. He removed the laptop, and then the papers, from within the bag and distributed them over his bed. James pointed at one of the pieces of paper.

'See, *The mirror is the key*'. And look…', James pressed the power key on the laptop. It started up, however the low battery symbol appeared in the corner of the screen. He knew he must be quick as in his rush to exit Nick's home he had not picked up the charger cable. 'I think Nick Sharp was the last person to see your wife. I found this laptop in Mr Sharp's house in the kitchen, along with a leather bag belonging to Sarah. Look, this is what he had shown your wife before she went missing, a slideshow of sorts- based around this myth… but maybe it isn't a myth! This woman, she… she must be the one who is taking all of the children that have gone missing. And that is why your daughter wrote you that message, to tell you that all of the children are being imprisoned in this orphanage.'

'That is a bit of a jump, don't you think?'

'More of a jump than believing that your daughter is communicating with you through the mirror in your house?'

Michael was silent to this. Instead he stroked the stubble that had formed around his face and gazed at the back of the mirror resting against the wall. James watched him, impatiently waiting for his response.

'Do you think Lucy was one of the children taken by this thing?'

'Yes! I think your daughter was one of the children this woman lured into her world! The mirrors. She must be able to get through via the mirrors. It sounds ridiculous but look at this.' James scrolled quickly through the Nick's PowerPoint, stopping every now and then to take in the information they held- as this was the first time he had seen what the presentation held. James keyed for the next slide. Just as the picture of 'The Smiling Woman' appeared on the screen, the last of the laptop's juice was exhausted and the screen went black.

'Who was that?'

'That, I think, is the thing that took Lucy. The thing that Sarah went in search for.'

Michael continued to stare at the black laptop screen, the image of the Woman burned into his eyes.

'How did Sarah go… Go to this other place?'

'I think using this…', James dipped his hand back into his bag and withdrew the small blue stone. Immediately, both of the men's eyes were locked to the stone.

'What is that? It's beautiful.' Michael said with adoration seeping from his voice.

'This is how we get your wife and daughter back… I think. I must confess, I know about as much information as you do now, but something drew me to this stone and I think, using these notes, that we can access 'the other side' somehow. It definitely said to go to the orphanage?'

'Definitely.'

'Orphanage… Is there an orphanage nearby?'

'No… Not one for miles around here…'

'Pass me your phone.'

Michael, without hesitation, passed James his mobile phone. James saw that he had several missed calls and unopened messages across the top of the screen. He opened up Google Maps and keyed in Stratford-upon-Avon- the location of Nick's house. It was a gut reaction, but as soon as the screen brought up the map, James knew it was the right one.

'There. The mirrors, the gateways, must open up at precise areas in the other world. There is an orphanage in Stratford, not far from where I met the thing disguised as Mr Sharp. I don't think it is a coincidence that Sarah was led to Mr Sharp, nor that the gateway she used to access the other world takes her to the exact location her child… your child… is being held captive. I think something more sinister is at work here. We need to get there, and quickly. Get my clothes, we will need to take your car.'

Chapter 15

Michael watched as the speedometer danced around the 70mph, as he drove towards Stratford-upon-Avon. James was sat in the seat next to him, typing frantically into his phone and reading through Nick's scrawled notes. Every now and again, James would take a sudden intake of breath, write something down into his own black notebook, and then continue to scroll through the internet. Each time Michael's eyes flicked to the rear-view mirror; he felt a cold chill run over his body.

'Was something watching them? Were they being led to a trap themselves?'

Michael felt his phone vibrate in his pocket.

'Must be the girlfriend… Boy have I got some explaining to do when I get home… If I get home. 'Where were you honey?' 'Oh just trying to rescue my ex-wife and dead daughter from another world, as they are being held captive by some scary-looking demon thing.' I am sure that would go down well!'

'Are you going to answer that?' James said from the passenger seat.

'No. I am better dealing with it all when this is over.' Although, Michael knew that she would suspect the worse if she found out he had visited his ex-wife- after seeing her only days before. She would assume seeing her re-ignited some flame from within and her imagination would take care of the rest.

'Watch your speed.'

'Hmm?'

'I said watch your speed. We don't want to get pulled over now.'

Michael nodded and brought his foot off the accelerator slightly. He thought back to the last time he had driven to Stratford-upon-Avon. It had been with Sarah and Lucy, for a Christmas treat. They had bought tickets to see a show at the RSC theatre- 'Twelfth Night'. A smile lifted the corners of his lips as he remembered how excited they had all been. The first time they had been to see a Shakespeare play, and it had not disappointed. They had come out after with linked arms, singing the play's finale song.

'What are you thinking about?'

James' voice broke Michaels' memory and his lips sank to their original shape they had become accustomed to.

'Nothing.'

'I think I have worked out how Nick managed to make contact with the other world. He has written a passage, a sort of ritual, on this piece of paper. I think- and I say think, because we are both entering a strange new world- but I think that if we recite these words next to the corresponding mirror, we can get Lucy back.'

'And Sarah?'

'Yes, and Sarah.' However, James kept his eyes away down as he said this- knowing that Sarah might have succumbed to the creatures on the other side. That, by the time they entered the other world, they may already be too late to save both of them.

After an hour of driving, that felt to Michael like three, they pulled up outside the orphanage in Stratford-upon-Avon. As they left the car, they couldn't help but think that they were at the wrong place. Rather than a feature of a horror movie, the building look well-kept and welcoming- quite the opposite of a home that housed the creepy, child catching demon.

The building held two large windows on the second floor, emitting an enticing, warm glow of life outwards. The welcoming light danced over the front garden that featured a kaleidoscope of colour. Red and white roses trailed up the newly painted fence, twisting around each other for comfort. Flowers of all kinds littered the ground around the gravel path to the front door like splashes of paint on the green canvas. Michael and James looked at each other, as if to say 'After you'. As the detective, James took the first step onto the gravelled path and crunched his way up to the front door-closely followed by Michael.

Before James pressed the doorbell, he could hear the joyful

laughter of children from within. He pressed down on the bell and heard the chimes echo around the building- even that sounded charming to the ear, as if joyfully letting the occupants know that they have visitors. The detective had often found that, like dogs and their owners, houses often imitated whom they belonged to. This house belonged to someone who spent their life caring for others, and no doubt inside would be equally well-kept.

'I'll get it!' a squeaky voice shouted from behind the door.

'Are you sure this is the right place?' Michael whispered, but before James could answer, the door opened and revealed a small, blonde girl with pigtails trailing down her back.

'Hiya, what can I do for you sirs?'

'Hi there little one. My name is detective... my name is James. Is there an adult I can speak to?'

'Sure', she turned around, 'Sonia! There is a detective here that wants to see you. You aren't trying to sell anything are you? Sonia hates people that sell door to door. Says it is... emvasif and most of them are a bunch of con-men.'

'Invasive. And no, we aren't selling anything I can assure you.' The little girl seemed content with this answer, but then her face turned serious- turning the adorable, freckled face of a little girl into that of a woman much older. 'Can I see your badge, mister?'

James smiled and reached into his pocket. 'Of course. Very wise, checking I am an actual detective.' He passed the badge down to the girl, whose face lit up as she looked at the badge.

'Do you have a gun mister?'

'No, I don't.' James said with a laugh.

'Have you ever killed anyone?'

'Not before visiting Mr Sharp's house... not before I was attacked by that thing.' Before he had to answer, 'Sonia' appeared behind the little girl.

'Thank you, Daisy.', Sonia said and looked nervously at the two men in her doorway. Daisy handed the badge back to James.

'See you mister. I hope you find your daughter.' She spun on her heels and ran back inside. Both men looked at each other with the same thought on her mind.

'Had either of us mentioned that?'

'How can I help you both?'

'Lovely kid.' James said- trying to get Sonia to warm to the visitors, before he asked to enter the building to enact a supernatural ritual that could well put all of the children under her care at risk.

'She is. What can I help you with?'

'My name is detective James Bannister, and this is my...colleague, Michael Bell.' Michael nodded towards Sonia. 'I was wondering if you would be able to help. Is there a mirror somewhere in this orphanage? A long, free-standing mirror would be ideal. I realise it is an odd question to ask, but it is rather urgent and very difficult to explain.'

Sonia's brow creased, as she looked at the two men before her- one with at least a day's worth of unshaven stubble spreading on his face, and the other with a bruise across his eye and stitches over a cut on his forehead. The pair must look as untrustworthy as a fox asking to be allowed into the chicken coop. It was Michael who broke the silence.

'I will make a large donation to your orphanage if you could please let us in. There are lives at stake. Please.'

Sonia contemplated this for a few minutes, that felt like a lifetime to the two men on the doorstep, but finally she moved to one side to let the two gentlemen into the orphanage.

'Thank you.' Michael said as he moved past her into the caring building, bringing only death and darkness with him.

After shutting the door, Sonia had said 'Follow me', and led them to the second floor of the building. As expected, the house was in immaculate condition and Michael expected that, had he ran a finger over the shelves, he would not have discovered a speck of dust or dirt. Not to say, however, that the house was in pristine condition- it had obviously been lived in, and that added a layer of character to the house that only children could provide. A quality which Michael's new house would never possess. As they moved through the house, children could be heard laughing behind close doors. Michael thought about the children who were at his daughter's sleepover the night his life changed. Thought about how they would have been laughing and joking, unsuspecting of the card fate had dealt them. Sonia walked to the end of the row of bedroom doors until she reached the final one. This door appeared different from the others, as if it had remained unused for years. Producing a keychain, Sonia selected a key with reluctance and inserted it into the lock of the door. After some effort (even the door wished to resist letting anyone inside) the door swung open with a creak, revealing the room within. It lay bare, apart from one object. A free-standing mirror lay on the far side, waiting.

'What do you want it for?'

'You wouldn't understand.' James muttered as he approached the mirror with caution.

'You would be surprised.' Sonia watched James with curiosity as he reached out and ran his finger across the mirror frame. 'I think it is haunted.'

'What makes you say that?' Michael asked- still standing by the doorway, away from the mirror's grasp.

'There have been a few incidents with the children- ', Sonia stopped herself mid-sentence, remembering that the man before her was a police detective.

'Go on.' James muttered under his breath as he continued his stand-off with the mirror. Sonia moved to the door and, after Michael had fully stepped inside the room, she closed it to confine the dark secrets to the ears of her visitors.

'The mirror was here when we bought the house to convert into an orphanage. The frame looked very expensive, and we thought maybe we could sell it. You know, to raise some funds to pay for other necessities. We had already put so much of our savings into the place, any amount of money would have helped. So, we advertised it, found a buyer, and then began planning how to post it to the buyer. The buyer was someone in America, so we had to book a removal team to package it and take it away. Two large men came to collect it, but the strange thing is- they couldn't move it. I mean, they couldn't physically move it. As if the frame was nailed into the floor. Refusing to give up, one of the men returned alone, armed with a hammer to prise the stand from the floor... We don't know exactly what happened. All I remember was that I was downstairs in the kitchen talking to the other removal man when I heard the scream of one of my children. I raced upstairs to find the man, right there.', Sonia pointed to the spot where James now stood, 'With the hammer... the hammer was embedded in his eye socket. And the worst thing was... he wasn't dead. His blooded hand held onto Daphne, one of our girls at the time, repeating two words over and over. 'The woman'.' James and Michael gave each other a knowing look, before Sonia continued. ' We called the police and the ambulance but by the time they arrived he was dead. The police thought he must have slipped or something but... Whatever had happened, the hammer had struck with so much force that it had smashed the back of his skull outwards. The only other thing in this room with him was that mirror. Ever since that incident, we have kept this room locked.'

'You said there have been incidents with the children?'

'Yes. At night, they hear voices coming from within here. Children's voices. Asking for help. Asking for their mother.' This sent a shiver down Michael's spine, knowing that the mother to his daughter had elected to take on this demonic force on her own, because the father hadn't wanted to believe her.

'Have you heard anything like this?'

Sonia shook her head, 'I haven't heard children's voices, but I don't think they are lying. The fear… the fear that is in their eyes, no one can fake. There was one thing… I was in bed one night asleep- I sleep just down the hall, so that if anything happens I can get to my children quickly- when I heard a loud bang. I shot out of bed and ran down the hall, thinking that one of the children had broken into this room or something. But the door remained locked and all of my children were still in bed. None of them had even woken up to the banging sound even. I thought perhaps I had dreamt it or something but then… I saw…I saw the handle… the handle on the door turned. Someone on the inside turned it. The next day I unlocked the room, but nothing was inside apart from that mirror. I haven't been in this room since that day… almost a year ago now. You must think I am crazy.'

'No. No I don't.' Michael looked towards James for permission to share their story with Sonia, to at least put her mind at ease that she wasn't crazy, but he shook his head. Sometimes it is better to let people believe the boogeyman is simply a story in their mind, not something that hides in the darkness under your bed.

'Thank you Miss, we will take it from here.'

Slightly taken aback by this sudden reluctance to share their story, Sonia nodded and left the room. Michael moved forward to stand next to James, their reflections standing side by side in the mirror, gazing back at them.

'Are you ready?' James' voice trembled slightly but his eyes remained confident. Michael tried to reply but resorted to nodding his head in response.

'Time to get your daughter back.'

Chapter 16

With the park behind her, Sarah now headed towards the orphanage- walking slowly but steadily- following the path of the river Avon. Knowing from the map that the orphanage lay on the path of the river, she must stay as close to it's course as possible. The water looked as black as oil, and seemed to glide without a current.

'I wonder what beasts lie beneath the surface…'

Every so often, she checked over her shoulder for any followers- whether clowns, Ravens or any other of the ungodly residents that roamed in this realm. However, so far, none had been spotted and she continued through the darkness to her destination. The thought of what had saved her from death at the hands of the clown plagued her mind.

'There are so many despicable creatures in this world, perhaps there are some forces for good?'

This contemplation was pushed out of her mind as she was forced to a halt by a large wooden fence blocking her path. On the fence a 'C' was drawn in a dark red, marking the end of the clown's territory. Sarah looked to her right, following the edge of the wall with her eyes. Approximately twenty metres down, she could see a small opening in the wall. Just as Sarah began to head that way, her mind drifted back to the spider's warning.

'Take the river… perhaps it is a trap…'

Gazing now to her left, Sarah could see a small wooden rowing boat moored to the edge of the river, bobbing up and down on the black water.

'Another coincidence! I can't believe I am trusting a talking spider.'

Sarah carefully put one foot into the boat, followed by the other- fearing the boat would capsize at any moment and throw her into the disgusting depths of the River Avon to the creatures below the surface. After balanced herself in the centre of the boat, she removed the rope from its mooring and waited for the boat to drift out from the path. Removing the oars from the base of the boat, she inserted them gently into the water and pulled. The boat moved forward slightly, then backwards under the force of the wave it had caused in the opaque water. With another stroke, it continued on it's journey up the River Avon and past the clown's barricade. The contrast of the peacefulness that the rowing had brought to Sarah's journey was not lost on her, and she took this time to plan her next steps.

'I'll row a bit further up the river, then follow the rest of the path to the church. It will be much quicker on foot. From there, I should be able to find my way to the orphanage and Lucy.'

Sarah's heart fluttered when the name came into her thoughts. The thought of being so close to holding her daughter again filled her with determination and confidence.

'Nothing can stand in my way.'

Bang.

A sound came from behind Sarah, seemingly from the barricade wall. The clowns had found their prisoner had escaped.

'Was that the clowns realising their meal has escaped?'

Sarah couldn't resist letting a smug smile creep onto her face- which quickly disintegrated into a look of worry as the boat rose and fell on the water. It remained still, and then the boat rose again and fell.

'There is something in this water. I knew it. There is something underneath me.'

Deciding that she had rowed enough (and being fearful of what lay beneath the water) she turned the boat and brought it back to the path on the edge of the river. After clambering onto the gravel path, she looked back over her shoulder into the depths but under the dark night sky Sarah could see nothing beneath the shimmering reflective surface. Looking to her right, the path from the barricade remained empty.

'The clowns must have given up catching their prey.'

For what felt like hours, Sarah walked along the riverbank until she saw a large black mass ahead through the darkness. Although she couldn't make out the features of the building; she could see a large cross prominently on the top of a wide speer.

'The church.'

The church was built of a grey stone and towered over the river and the other houses beside it, a symbol of safety even in this world. As Sarah reached the small wooden fence that bordered the perimeter of the churchyard, she reached out her hand to touch the rough wood. The church had given her hope. She was close.

There was a small archway leading from the path into the churchyard and, Sarah knew from the map, there would be one that exited the area on the other side of the church. The path leading towards the archway was guarded with large willow trees bending inwards, protecting those who pass through, sheltering the visitors under their leaves.

'There she is!'

Spinning round on her heels, Sarah saw five horrifying clowns, saliva dribbling from their mouths, running up the path towards her. Without thinking, she stepped backwards, through the archway and into the churchyard. Moving backwards, with her eyes never leaving her pursuers, she was nearly at the end of the willow tree guard line when the clowns screeched to a halt. They looked down at their feet, each had lined up perfectly with the archway that led into the churchyard- not one placing a toe over the line. The clowns muttered to each other, so that Sarah couldn't hear what was being said, and then the middle clown in the line up held out a dirty, white gloved hand.

'Come with us. We will kill you quickly. You will wish you had listened. Come with us. It will be a better ending for you, better than what she has planned.'

Sarah looked again at how they had formed a line the other side of the archway.

'They are scared of this place! They can't bring themselves to cross the threshold- like vampires unable to enter a person's home without permission.'

'And why would I do that? You bastards can starve!' Sarah's voice echoed through the trees, aimed directly at her pursuers. A sense of confidence had risen in her, knowing that she was safe within the walls of the church.

'Shhh! You don't know where you are! You don't know what is waiting for you. Come here, before it is too late!'

'Fuck you!'

The clowns shook their heads and muttered something between each other again, just quiet enough to not reach Sarah's ears. They took one last look at their prey, turned, and made their slow way- back to their park Sarah presumed. Once they had moved out of sight, Sarah turned back to face the church that stood resolutely before her, relief flooding through her bones.

'At least holy ground is still sacred in this world.'

Sarah had never been a religious person, in fact she often openly mocked those who dedicate their life to following the teachings of the bible. However, as she gazed upon the aged brickwork of the church, a wave of holiness coursed through her blood. A feeling of safety within the church's grounds, away from the cursed beings that inhabited this world. She could thank nobody for that feeling of safety, other than God.

As she walked around the gravel path that marked the outskirts of the church, she reached her hand out to the wall and felt the cold, rough brick under her fingertips. The building appeared empty, vacated long ago, as moss and weeds emerged from the cracks in the stone and the stained glass windows were dark and uncleaned.

'How long had this church stood here? Protecting wandering travellers?'

The feeling of peace and safety left Sarah's body as quickly as it had entered. She had been mistaken. It had not been the holy ground that had protected her from the clowns that had chased her. Quite the opposite in fact. It had been the fear they had of what lay within the fenced area. Fear of what now stood before her in the graveyard.

The graveyard was littered with disintegrating gravestones marking the forgotten dead beneath. At first sight, the figures that stood next to these gravestones could have been mistaken as statues. That is until Sarah noticed the long, curved black beaks. As soon as her boot made contact with the gravel, every nightmarish Raven that lurked in the graveyard turned it's head toward the intruder on their land. Remaining motionless, hoping that they may mistake her for a statue in the dim light, she held her breath. For a moment, she believed that it worked. For a moment, she believed that there may have been a way out of the situation she found herself in. But that moment didn't last long.

What proceeded felt to Sarah like it was acted in slow motion and lasted for hours, but actually occurred in a matter of seconds. Her weight shifted to the foot that had alerted the guarding Ravens and she pushed off, scattering gravel onto the grass that surrounded the path, and darted in the opposite direction. Knowing that if she followed the gravel path around the border of the church, she would reach the gate that led out of the yard. Every sense in her body felt electrified, every sound felt intensified in her head and every second felt like a lifetime. Without looking behind her, she heard the Ravens close in- not from the sound of their boots on the gravel, but from the feeling of impending doom in her heart. Her foot slid on the gravel as she turned another corner of the church wall and a hand reached out to steady herself, grazing down the wall. She gripped her fingernails into the rough stone and propelled herself forward. Straight ahead of her, she could see the gate under the archway.

What if they didn't stop their chase once she was out of the churchyard? What if the clowns had circled back, knowing I would need to escape through this exit? What if- '

This thought remained unfinished in her head, as she felt a pain in her right shoulder that froze all of her muscles. Sarah let out a scream as the pain in her shoulder intensified. It was a hand, a claw, digging it's razor sharp claws into her flesh. An unholy force thrust her body to the gravelled floor like a rag doll and caused her scream out again. Sarah looked towards the archway, the archway that had seemed so close, before looking up at her attacker. The last image Sarah saw was of a Raven standing above her, it's curved beak pointing down at it's captured prey. Then, nothing.

Chapter 17

Detective James Bannister and Michael stood at opposite sides of the room in the orphanage, with the mirror standing ominously between them. James had a sheet of paper in his hand, covered in scrawled handwriting from their car ride over. Michael held the stone.

'Can we hurry? This stone… It is making me feel…'

'What?'

'Powerful.' James looked from the paper to Michael- who was staring at the stone in his palm, as if in a trance.

'I think I'm ready. Remember, keep the stone in your hand at all times. Do not drop it.' Michael nodded in response, barely hearing what James had actually said.

'Had his ex-wife held the stone and felt the same power surging from it?'

James coughed into his hand to clear his throat, and then began.

'Forces of the night. We call to you for your help. We bow to your knowledge and ask for your assistance. Please, hear us.'

Silence.

'Forces of the night, please hear us. Come to us.'

Silence.

'Maybe this isn't working…' Michael muttered.

'Forces of the night! Come to us! Now!'

The electric lights in the room flickered and then went out, leaving the two in complete darkness.

'Forces, are you here with us?'

'I'm heeeeeere.'

The temperature in the room plummeted as both Michael and James looked from the mirror, to the corner of the room where the croaking voice had come from. A light came from the shadows, the light of a match being struck. Michael could see the match rise to light a long, fat cigar. This was confirmed by a puff of smoke that then filled the air.

'Who is it that brought me here?'

Both of the men remained silent.

'If you are going to waste my time, I will go.' The thing's voice was low and gravely.

'It was me. I brought you here. Asked you here. We need your help.' It was Michael that forced these words from his mouth, as James remained mute with fear.

'Of course you want my help. What do you want? I don't have all day.'

'We need to access another world through this mirror. A world where there is a woman… a woman who is taking children.' The thing stopped smoking and removed the cigar from his mouth, briefly lighting his face- however, Michael only saw the black coal eyes that glinted in the embers.

'Another one? I have already helped one man and a woman travel into this world… It didn't end well for the man… And I doubt the woman will fare much better', the thing chuckled to himself, 'There is a fee, you understand. I require something from you. Something valuable, that you cannot get back. A deal such as this is final and the debt must be paid. Years.'

'What do you mean? Years?' James spoke this time- finding the courage to force his mouth to move.

'The other man was better prepared than you… Much better prepared. Listen carefully to what I about to say. Remember that once the contract is agreed to, the debt must be paid. I require years from your life. These years can be taken from anywhere within your life, you will never know from where I have taken them. These may be years taken from your current life, in which case you will lose all memories from that period. It may be the last years of your life, cutting your allocated time in this world short. Ten years should suffice. Each.' Michael and James looked at each other, unsure about what to say or do next.

'Is it a deal or not? I have other places to be.' The creature in the corner puffed again on the cigar, sending clouds of smoke puffing into the room. Michael spoke first.

'Deal.'

'Wait, Michael, are you sure-'

'I am getting my daughter back! If you want to leave, I won't hold it against you. But I am not leaving this place without my daughter. Deal.' James felt the creature's coal eyes move to him, watching intently to see whether he would be collecting two debts or one.

'Deal.'

'Goooooood. When the time is right, you will be able to enter. Use the stone to pass between the worlds- but be quick. It won't last long.' The figure put the cigar back into his mouth and breathed in deeply. Two fingers emerged in front of the cigar's flaming embers.

Snap.

The electric lights flickered back on. The thing was gone.

'What do we do now?' Michael asked.

'We wait.'

Chapter 18

Thud.

Sarah's head hit the pavement with enough force to compel her eyes open. The first sensation that filled her body was that of fear. Fear was replaced quickly with pain shooting from her feet. It was that moment Sarah realised that she was moving- being dragged forwards by her feet. By lowering her eyes, she saw two Ravens with their claws latched around her ankles. They must have felt the shift of weight under their talons as she woke, but their attention remained focused on dragging the body towards a destination unknown to Sarah.

'Are they taking me back to the clowns?'

Sweat trickled down Sarah's face, diluting the blood that clung to her forehead above her brow, and dripped to the pavement beneath her. In her helplessness, her mind drifted to the tail of Hansel and Gretel leaving breadcrumbs to ensure they could find their way out of the dark wood. Sarah dreaded to think what creatures may follow her trail of blood...

The Ravens came to a stop simultaneously and without communication. Her feet were released, and hit the pavement, which sent another shot of pain up her legs. Sarah tried to raise her head to look at the kidnappers, but they were gone. Not a Raven in sight. Like a parcel, Sarah had been left at it's destination for it's recipient to collect. Pushing her hands beneath her, she raised her body and looked over her feet to see where she had been left.

The image before her was as if from a dream, because it was. Before Sarah was the actualisation of her nightmare only a few days before. A few days that felt like years. A rusty gate creaked in the wind, resting on one loose hinge. Beyond the gate, a gravel path, weeds peering through the stone covering- desperately trying to see sunlight that never shone. Sarah's eyes followed the path up to the weathered brown door. Above the door was a hand painted sign. In a dark scarlet, it read 'Orphanage'.

Forgetting the pain in her legs, Sarah used the gate to bring herself to her feet. Thankfully, the gate stood strong against her weight and she now stood before the path. Heartbeat quickening, temple throbbing, hands shaking; Sarah pushed the gate open and placed her first foot onto the gravel. In her mind's eye, she could see the serpent weeds taking life and wrapping around her ankles- but they remained silent and still. Instead choosing to watch the wounded gazelle walk freely into the lion's trap. As if the Smiling Woman had heard these thoughts, the door to the Orphanage slowly swung open and beckoned Sarah in with open arms. Wood chips hung from the top of the door frame like stalagmites in a cave... or teeth. Now, without control of her feet, Sarah found herself climbing the small step and before she knew it she stood before the doorway peering in.

That was the moment Sarah heard it. At first, she thought it was the wind. Perhaps the creak of the old gate. But no. It was one word that echoed faintly from within the mouth house. One word that gave Sarah all the strength she needed to step beyond the door and into the shadowy lair within.

'Mummy!'

Chapter 19

Sarah rushed through the door. As she did, something slammed it behind her, locking her inside. But Sarah barely noticed, her focus was purely in front of her. Her task- to find her daughter.

The house resembled a forgotten, derelict care home. Empty photo frames littered the walls and were covered with a blanket of dust.

'Mummy.' It came from the somewhere up the stairs. Grasping the paint-chipped bannister for support, she climbed the stairs to reach the top floor of the house. With each step, the room felt colder- confirming to Sarah that she was heading in the right direction.

At the top of the stairs lay a long corridor led down the centre of the house with rooms leading off- each door appearing old and weathered. At the end of the corridor, a black door. This door was freshly painted, and the black gloss shone even with no light to reflect. Sarah moved swiftly down the corridor to the first room. The door lay open, revealing a small, dim candle-lit room containing one single bed. The damp smell of mould and dirt met Sarah with such force that she had struggled to maintain her balance. However, as she did so, she noticed a small figure in the corner of the room, sat with their back facing the door. The figure's back was moving up and down as the person held back tearful sobs.

'Hello?'

The figure's back stopped still. Even though the light was dim, Sarah could make out the features of the face as the person turned towards the door. A small girl. Her face was dirty and wet with tears.

'Have you come to help me?' Sarah didn't know how to reply. Part of her wanted to tell the little girl that her prime goal was to find her own daughter. However, the mother in her heart wouldn't let such things leave her mouth- even though she hadn't been a mother for many years.

'Yes... Yes, I have come to help you. Where are the others?'

The little girl leapt towards Sarah and within a second her arms were wrapped around this stranger that had entered her closet sized room. The mother felt her arms enclosing around the little girl, bringing her in tight. A natural instinct that she had not experienced since her daughter was taken. Tears welled up in Sarah's eyes, stinging until she had to release one arm from around the child to wipe her eyes.

'Where are the others?'

'Down there. Behind the last door.'

Sarah went to leave but was held in place by the little girl small hand in her's.

'Please come back.' the little girl whispered.

'I promise.'

The girl let Sarah go with a new smile on her face that brought beauty to the dirty, starved child. With that, Sarah turned back to the door at the end of the corridor. A corridor that seemed longer since she last looked down it. The tap of her shoes on the wooden floor seemed amplified in the silence to sound like cannons firing. Five steps away from the door.

Is Lucy behind it?'

Four steps away from the door.

Will she remember me?'

Three steps away from the door.

What if her kidnapper is behind the door? The Smiling Woman?'

Two steps away from the door. Sarah's mind travelled back to the pictures of the Smiling Woman. Her lips stretched across her cheeks.

One step-

The door swung open.

Before Sarah could back away, a pale white taloned hand shot from the darkness, wrapped around Sarah's face, and pulled her within.

Chapter 20

The Smiling Woman sat in a large throne centred in her cavernous lair. The throne, at first glance, appeared like it was constructed from ivory. However, on closer inspection, it was revealed that the throne was in fact made from teeth. Children's teeth. The Smiling Woman wore a black shawl that hung over her greasy hair. In hand, a silver staff, entwined with an oaken wood that coiled from base to top.

Behind the throne were three rows of four wooden chairs. In each, a dishevelled prisoner, some barely five years old, others older- the oldest had a streak of grey hair laying amongst the black, uncut strands. Chains wrapped around each of the prisoners' ankles and wrists so tightly they left bruises where they rested. The remains of the room appeared empty, other than six mirrors fastened to each of the six walls in the hexagonal domain. Before the throne, lying unconscious on the glistening opaque floor, was the mother of a kidnapped child.

The Smiling Woman raised her staff above the floor and brought it down with a tap that boomed throughout the chamber, forcing Sarah to awaken.

'Welcome back.' The Smiling Woman sneered with a grotesque satisfaction. Sarah looked up into the Smiling Woman's eyes, the eyes of the creature that had taken her daughter from her. Anger filled her but all she could do was kneel before the throne. The prisoner's hopeless eyes remained fixed on the floor with realisation that their rescuer had failed. The Smiling Woman tilted her head slightly, watching Sarah as a visitor watches an animal in a zoo. Waiting to see what the animal might do next to entertain them. Sarah twisted her body to free herself from the force that pushed her to the floor, but to no avail. She was trapped.

'What a pity… I thought you had more fight in you than that…'. The voice sent shivers through Sarah's body. The Smiling Woman raised a taloned hand and snapped her fingers. From behind the white throne, chains fell from one of her prisoners.

'Come.'

The freed prisoner remained motionless, staring at the floor.

'I said come!'

The prisoner stood cautiously and limped towards the Smiling Woman. Sarah could see the prisoner, a young teenager, had a deep cut travelling diagonally from her left eye to the corner of her lip. Over her head, the prisoner wore a dirtied bedsheet with a hole cut in the centre. Her feet were bare and bloodied, causing her to wince with every step she took. The young woman's eyes flicked from the floor to Sarah's. Eyes that Sarah would have recognised anywhere, because any mother would. Tears welled and poured from her eyes, her lips quivered, and her throat seemed to seal up with love.

'Lucy?'

'Mum?'

Although she was older, Sarah knew without any doubt she was hers. Sarah moved to rise, to scoop her daughter up in her arms and cover her with all the owed kisses that the years had stolen, but the Smiling Woman raised her hand and a tremendous force pushed Sarah to her knees once more. The Woman moved a clawed hand to Lucy and gently caressed the side of her cheek with a razor-sharp talon. Lucy winced as the sharp point sliced into her skin with ease.

'Don't you hurt her!' Sarah screamed.

'Why would I hurt my daughter?' Her smile widened as her attention fixed back to the woman before her. 'She was so pretty… So pretty when I found her. Time does come for us all… Takes our beauty from us. Doesn't it my dear?' Lucy turned her head away from the Smiling Woman, but the razor-sharp nails dug into her chin and turned it back towards her. 'Ah, ah. Let's not misbehave when we have a guest. You wouldn't want to be punished again, would you?'

'What do you want? I will give you anything, just please let her go' Sarah wept- still trying with all her might to rise against the debilitating force pushing her into the ground.

'Anything? That is a large promise… A promise I am not sure you can keep.'

'Please, I will. I will do anything to have my daughter back'. At the word daughter, the Smiling Woman's face changed. Her skin became warmer and her eyes changed to a dark blue Sarah had seen before. The colour of the stone. Her whole demeanour altered from standing proudly above her capture, to bending slightly in guilt.

'I don't have much time. There is a darkness within… A darkness within me that I cannot control for much longer. I have been watching you. You are… different. Different from the others. I had begun to lose hope that another would arrive. I have taken many, many children… From those many parents I have stolen their child, only a few have entered this world…You thought you were the first? No… Out of those few that made the journey, only one has survived… and here you are. With some help.' The Smiling Woman laughed.

'What do you mean?'

'Do you think it a coincidence that your dream showed you the exact location of my lair? Or that you happened to find the one stone that could bring you to this world? What do you think those hideous clowns are so scared of, that they leave the first meal they have seen in months? I thought you were smarter…'

Sarah looked into the eyes of her capturer and realisation dawned upon her who had been her saviour in the circus tent, who had guided her to the rowing boat, and who had orchestrated her whole journey so that she arrived at the orphanage in one piece. However, as Sarah stared into the face of the Smiling Woman, she saw not the face that had been captured in the pictures Nick Sharp had shown her only days before, but another woman. The Smiling Woman nodded.

'I am not the first, nor will not be the last.'

'What is your name?'

'It has been so many years since someone has called me by it, I do not know anymore. I now have many names throughout the world. Names are important. Without the right name, something could be made nothing. My names inspire fear in the hearts of children throughout your world- I do not need another. We, the chosen, are cursed to entice the young into our world for the higher power. Forever travelling between worlds to steal the sons and daughters from their mothers, fulfilling the promise made by the first of our kind to the higher power all those years ago.'

'Who is the higher power?'

'Ah… there is much you don't understand and not enough time to tell it. You think you have seen horror in this world, but you haven't seen the half of what is out there. The universe is far more complicated than your little brain can comprehend. I rule this world, but there are many others like this. Alternate realities that are layered like pieces of paper, each balanced delicately next to the other. A tear in the paper, in the fragment of that world, can allow transference between them. I have the ability to create tears in the fabric of time and space- given to me by the higher power.'

'What happened to this world?'

'This world is one of many alternates to the one you call home. One alternate choice in the course of history can spiral a world into disaray. I was not in my position when that choice was made, but the beings that remain are…were… human. The poison in the air have mutated their genes, transformed them into the creatures you have seen.'

'Is that poison within me?' The Smiling Woman considered this question, but moved on from it.

'To answer your previous question, no one has seen the being who rules over all of the worlds. We all, however, obey his instruction. As I have said, I am cursed to bring children into this world for eternity.'

'Why are you telling me all of this?'

'Because Sarah Bell, there is a way out. A way to end my duty. This position cannot go un-filled, there must be an appointed ruler of this world. Do you understand? To leave, I must find another. One who willingly takes the throne from their predecessor. The same as I did, and the woman before me. And now you.'

'Why would I do take your place? Why would I curse myself to be like… like you?'

'Ah. I asked my predecessor the same question… many years ago. There are many reasons why one would take on this curse. Some desire power, to live for eternity. Some wish to cause pain and suffering by harming ones that others love. I…Let me show you.'

The Smiling Woman raised a hand to one of the six mirrors and snapped her taloned fingers. The mirror shimmered, then sprung into life- turning from a mirror into a window. Through this lay an elderly man lying on a white hospital bed. His eyes lids were closed but fluttered gently as he breathed in and out using the ventilator at the side of his bed.

'That man is my son. He was... taken from me... He was only four when she took him. I would do anything to have him back. As you know, it is a mother's duty to look after her child. I made the same journey you have done, only when I arrived at this orphanage, I was given a choice. My son's life for mine. He would be returned to my world if I stayed in this one, to continue as the heir to the throne.' The Smiling Woman waved her hand and the image disappeared. 'I will give the same choice to you. Your life, for your daughter's. My son has lived his life. When I have moments of... clarity... when the darkness within is concealed, I have been able to observe him as he has grown older. Now, his life... his beautiful life... is nearly at it's end. I am ready to move on to whatever is next. However, the position must be filled. To take a life, one must give it. I am giving you that chance. Take it.'

Sarah's mouth dried so that she could barely make a sound. Her eyes moved from the Smiling Woman to Lucy.

'Don't do it Mum.'

'Lucy I-'

'Mum... please... don't.'

Sarah took a deep breath and licked her lips. Whatever answer came from her lips would change her future forever. But she knew there was only one choice a mother could make.

'I'll do it.'

'No! Mum! No!'

The Smiling Woman's grin widened once more, the sparkling blue disappearing from her eyes and her rotting teeth filling the dark space between the lips.

'Take her.'

Ravens marched in from the walls where they had been concealed with the shadows. Two fastened their hands onto Sarah's shoulders, another grasped her head and brought it back so that she faced the ceiling above. The Smiling Woman rose from her chair with silent grace and descended upon her successor. As the Smiling Woman glided towards Sarah, her hand moved beneath the shawl to remove a thin shard of glistening, black glass. Sarah tried to move her head against the Raven's strong claws but before she could blink, the glass had slid to the right corner of her lips.

'Now… smile.'

Sarah tried to shout, tried to scream, but the glass slid effortlessly through her cheek. Blood filled her mouth and poured down her shirt onto the floor. The hand wielding the weapon turned and slid the opposite direction. However, this time the glass's jagged edge caught on Sarah's skin. Without hesitation, the Smiling Woman pushed with more force and it continued on its path. The energy drained from her body. Her eye's flicked to Lucy, who stood horrified, watching her mother sacrifice herself to save her daughter. The mother wanted to say 'I love you', wanted to say 'This isn't your fault. Live your life. Be happy.' but the only sound that emerged was that of gurgling blood in her throat. Then-

Chapter 21

'Sarah! Lucy!'

The Ravens holding Sarah released their grasp and turned to the sound. Shocked, the Smiling Woman lowered her glass wielding hand. The centre mirror on the wall had transformed into a doorway, through which stood Detective James Bannister and Michael Bell.

'No!', the Smiling Woman shrieked with such force the room began to tremble under it's might, 'No!'

'Lucy! Sarah! Quickly! We don't have much time!'

Lucy began to run towards her father but the Smiling Woman had seen her and was already moving to intercept.

Pain soared through Sarah's face, her brain trying to comprehend what was happening, her body shaking under the shock. Time seemed to slow as the Smiling Woman glided towards Lucy with her one arm outstretched to seize the prisoner.

'She was never going to let my daughter go.'

Sarah's eyes fixed upon the Smiling Woman's other hand. Summoning all of her might, Sarah rose from the floor, pushed her way through the Ravens and launched herself at the Smiling Woman. Their bodies collided, forcing the Smiling Woman to the floor. Sarah grappled for the shard of glass in the Woman's hand and found it. Raising the glass above her head, her eyes never leaving the Smiling Woman's, her blooded teeth emerged in a sneer. Through the pain and blood pouring from her mouth, she gurgled two words.

'Die Bitch!'

Sarah brought the glass down with such force the point of the shard sliced straight through the bridge of the Smiling Woman's nose and buried itself deep in her skull. The surrounding Ravens unleashed a terrifying howl in unison, each one falling to the floor with grief for their fallen leader.

'Sarah! Quick! Come on!'

Sarah looked towards the mirror, seeing the two people she loved most in this world. Safe.

'The curse…' Sarah looked down at the Smiling Woman whose lips twitched with each word being uttered from those horrific lips. 'You must…stay… for them…The seat must… be filled…' The twitching stopped. Sarah watched as the face of the Smiling Woman, the face that had horrified and haunted children around the world for so many years, cracked like a porcelain doll. The final crack appeared. The Smiling Woman's face crumbled from within, leaving only the black shawl in her place. A shawl without an owner. Although, in her heart, Sarah knew this wasn't true. The mother had been brought here for a reason, not by the Smiling Woman, but by the higher power.

'Come on!' Michael was reaching out of the mirror, his arm outstretched for Sarah to take. She looked back at the shawl beneath her, looked at the Ravens kneeling around her in despair, and then to the love of her life. Through her cut lips, Sarah smiled.

'I love you.'

With a wave of Sarah's hand, the window transformed back to a mirror. Michael and Lucy were gone.

Lucy was safe.

Lucy was home.

Part Three

Chapter 22

'Vampires. Many believe vampires to be like that in fiction; handsome and charming with a swirling black cloak and pointed teeth. Although some truth can be found in these tales; most of it is... well most of it is crap.'. The students in the lecture hall let out a small chuckle. 'In my experience, vampires need to be feared more than those in books and films. For, in real life, vampires look just like you and me. They can walk about in daylight, go to pubs and nightclubs, even attend lectures. Instead of bursting into flames in sunlight, or glittering like a disco ball, they wear a skin-tight outfit made of... well, skin. They can be anyone they wish to be. Driven by lust, they either want to kill you or fuck you. There is no in-between. If ever you encounter one, your best course of action is to run. Run and don't look back.'

A hand rises in the mass of students.

'Yes?'

'Hi. Yes. Thank you, Miss Bell. I just have two quick questions. You said, 'in my experience'... does that mean you have met a vampire? And to follow on from that, was it a vampire that left that scar on your face?'. Miss Bell's hand reached up to her face and followed the scar line.

'No. This scar is from... from something much worse. And as

for the vampires, I haven't just met a vampire. I have met many. But that is a story for another day as unfortunately, we have come to the end of this slot. Thank you all so much for your time. My email is in the leaflet I think, so I will be more than happy to reply to any queries.'

The students applauded and then started the fight to exit the lecture hall through two small doors at the rear. Miss Lucy Bell looked down at her mobile on the desk. A text message alert was bouncing on the screen. She slid her finger across it to reveal the text.

'I hope the lecture went well today. Your mother and I are so proud of you. And Happy Birthday! Who'd have thought it! 38! You are nearly getting as old as me. :D *Let me know when you get home. Dad XX'*

Lucy read it through once and then chucked her phone into her rucksack. 'Mother'. That woman had relished the opportunity to take over from where Lucy's actual mother had left off.

After Lucy had returned to this world, in a week her father had completely forgotten about the Smiling Woman. Forgot how his ex-wife had stayed in the other world. Detective James Bannister had informed her that as part of a 'deal with the devil', her father had sacrificed 10 years of his life. The 'devil' had chosen to take the memory of Lucy's mother- leaving Michael with gaps of empty space in his memories where she used to be. Perhaps this was a blessing in disguise, for her father at least. For Lucy, this had created a divide between herself and her father. Leaving her to cry alone in the night, when she misses her mother terribly and holds her stuffed teddy bear close.

Slinging the rucksack over her shoulder, she walked through the University campus. Her watch told her it was almost half two. Just time for a toilet break and a coffee before she drove home. She found her way to the toilets and pushed open the door, keeping her head down as the last thing she wanted was to be bombarded by questions when she was on the toilet.

Lucy finished her business and moved up to the sink to wash her hands. The lights flickered. Lucy looked around the empty room. Experience had taught her that the things from the other side waited for no one- not even for people to wash their hands. She returned her attention to the sink and washed her soapy hands in the cold water running from the hot tap. Until she saw an object wrapped around the cold tap. A thin, golden chain connected to a locket.

Opening it, Lucy found a picture inside of her father and herself staring back. A memory frozen in time within the locket.

Tap.

Tap.

Tap.

Lucy's heart froze. Slowly, she looked up into the mirror. Before her stood a woman. A scarlet smile cut into her cheeks, her white eyes sunken into her face and her hair lay lifeless down the side of her pale white face. The woman in the mirror smiled and tilted her head slightly.

'Mother?'

The End

ABOUT THE AUTHOR

M.A. Edwards is best known for his debut play In The Shadows which was published by Olcan Press in 2022. The Smiling Woman is M.A. Edwards' debut novel and Olcan is delighted to have partnered again to bring this fabulous piece of work to life.

For more information and to see our entire catalogue of publications head to olcan.co.
.

Printed in Great Britain
by Amazon

12225182R00091